SPIN-OFFS AND EQUITY CARVE-OUTS

Achieving Faster Growth and
Better Performance

James A. Miles and J. Randall Woolridge
The Pennsylvania State University

A publication of Financial Executives Research Foundation, Inc.

Financial Executives Research Foundation, Inc.
10 Madison Avenue
P.O. Box 1938
Morristown, NJ 07962-1938
(973) 898-4608

International Standard Book Number 1–885065–14–0
Library of Congress Catalog Card Number 98–073869
Printed in the United States of America

First Printing

Financial Executives Research Foundation, Inc. (FERF®) is the research affiliate of Financial Executives Institute. The basic purpose of the Foundation is to sponsor research and publish informative material in the field of business management, with particular emphasis on the practice of financial management and its evolving role in the management of business.

The views set forth in this publication are those of the authors and do not necessarily represent those of the FERF Board as a whole, individual trustees, or the members of the Advisory Committee.

FERF publications can be ordered by calling 1-800-680-FERF
(U.S. and Canada only; international orders, please call 770-751-1986).
Quantity discounts are available.

Cover design by Mark Tocchet.

CONTENTS

Introduction

As companies revamp their organizational and ownership structures to become more competitive, it is clear that the restructuring movement of the 1990s—especially spin-offs and equity carve-outs (ECOs)—has greatly changed the corporate landscape.

Spin-offs involve the divestment of a business division to shareholders through a distribution of the subsidiary's common stock in the form of a dividend. In most cases, the spin-off is structured to be a tax-free distribution to both the parent and investors. Notable spin-offs include Quaker Oats–Fisher Price Toys, Adolph Coors–ACX Technologies, General Motors–EDS, Pacific Telesis–Air Touch, and Union Carbide–Praxair.

In an ECO, a parent sells equity in a subsidiary to the public in the form of an initial public offering (IPO). In most cases, the parent retains a majority equity stake in the subsidiary. ECOs also have grown significantly and have included AT&T–AT&T Capital, Textron–Paul Revere, as well as Thermo Electron (TE) and its many carve-outs, including Thermolase, Thermo Instrument, and Thermo Fibertek. And finally, there have been numerous ECO/spin-off combinations. These divestments, often called spin-outs or two-stage spin-offs, involve an ECO in a subsidiary, followed by a spin-off of the parent's remaining equity interest. Notable two-stage spin-offs include AT&T–Lucent Technologies, Sears Roebuck–Allstate Insurance, and Pacific Telesis–Air Touch.

Motivations for spin-offs and ECOs vary. Sometimes a combination of businesses may be perceived as undervalued by the market. This perception may be due to a lack of synergy between the parent and subsidiary or between business units, to the market's poor understanding of the combined entity, or to the excessive operating volatility of one of the entities. Sometimes separating a subsidiary from other business units is useful for strategic, human resource, or financing reasons. Generally, if alternative units require different strategies for success, if they require different managerial talents (i.e., entrepreneurial versus tight controls), or if they have dissimilar capital and financing requirements, a separation may be beneficial. Finally, separation through spin-offs or ECOs can eliminate inefficient cross subsidies and lead to a more focused organization in which operating performance and compensation are more closely matched.

We have conducted a number of studies on spin-offs and ECOs. Our research demonstrates that these restructuring forms lead to superior operating results and stock performance for the subsidiaries involved.

In this study, we provide an in-depth look at spin-offs, ECOs, and two-stage spin-offs, describing the critical success factors for parent firms and subsidiaries. We discuss the background and technical details of these transactions, the tax and regulatory issues, the motivations for performing the transactions, and the research on the performance and valuation issues. The book also contains case studies of spin-offs and carve-outs.

Spin-Offs

Spin-offs have become the method of choice in the 1990s for companies seeking to deconglomerate and focus on core businesses. Normally, the business being spun off is non-core and is not the crown jewel of the parent company. But because of the increased size of spin-offs and the associated business media coverage, investors have shown more interest in them.

In a pure spin-off, a parent firm's shareholders receive a pro rata distribution of a wholly owned subsidiary's newly traded stock. For example, in Tenneco's 1996 spin-off of Newport News Shipbuilding, Tenneco's shareholders received one share of Newport News Shipbuilding for every five of their Tenneco shares. The net result is that, at the time of the distribution, the ownership structure of the spin-off is identical to that of the parent.[1] A spin-off effectively removes the parent from management and control of the subsidiary.

Standex International's 1981 stock distribution of its wholly owned subsidiary Bingo King Co. is a good example. Standex, primarily a refrigeration concern, announced its intention to spin off Bingo King, the leading U.S. manufacturer of bingo equipment, on September 9. The stated reason for the spin-off was to enable investors to participate more directly in Bingo King's growth and to provide greater visibility and investor interest for Standex. The 100-percent tax-free distribution was made on December 8 (ex-date: November 23; record date: November 30), with shareholders of Standex receiving one share of Bingo King for every five shares owned. Initial prices for spin-offs are determined in the market, and Bingo King began trading on a when-issued basis at $3.00 per share on November 23 on the over-the-counter (OTC) market. The stock price of Standex declined $.375 on the ex-date to reflect the distribution, giving Standex and Bingo King total market values of $92.7 million and $4.1 million, respectively.

In the following sections, we examine important aspects of spin-offs, including taxes, Securities and Exchange Commission (SEC) filing requirements and initial pricing, reasons for spin-offs, and relevant prior research. We also outline reasons why spin-offs may offer unusually high returns to investors.

Tax Status

A spin-off is considered a dividend by U.S. tax authorities. However, this dividend can be tax free to shareholders if the spin-off meets the criteria in Section 355 of the Internal Revenue Code (IRC), which include the following:

- Active conduct of business: Both the parent and the subsidiary must be engaged in an active trade or business for at least five years before the distribution date.

- Control: The parent must have control of the subsidiary before the spin-off (usually 80 percent of the voting stock), and the distribution must constitute at least 80 percent of the outstanding shares of the subsidiary. In addition, any shares retained by the parent must not constitute "practical control" of the subsidiary.

- Business purpose: The transaction may not be used as a means of distributing profits and must be done for a sound business reason. This reason must be business-related and not tied to shareholder interests. (Enhancing shareholder value is not a valid business reason.) Typical business reasons include complying with antitrust and other laws, allowing key employees to participate in company ownership, enhancing capital market access and financing opportunities, alleviating management differences, and disposing of unwanted assets.

Spin-offs are typically structured to meet these criteria, and parent firms frequently seek an opinion on the tax status of a proposed spin-off prior to distributing the shares.

Filing Requirements and Initial Pricing

Filing requirements with the SEC vary with the specific circumstances of the spin-off. The Exchange Act of 1934 requires, in most cases, that the parent firm file a Form 10 with the SEC. (Form 10 includes much of the information required to register an IPO in Form S-1.) The parent must provide standard historic financial information for the spin-off as well as unaudited financial statements showing the impact of the spin-off on the parent and the subsidiary. Shares in the subsidiary can be distributed only after the Form 10 becomes effective.

Prior to 1969, registration requirements for security sales imposed by the Securities Act of 1933 did not apply to spin-offs, which were considered dividends by the SEC. This situation led to allegations that shell companies were being created to acquire private firms and spin them off without registering the acquired firm's stock (Schipper and Smith, 1983). In Release 8909 (1970), the SEC required registration or disclosure of equivalent information if the stock of the divested subsidiary was to be traded (Schipper and Smith, 1983). Thus, Release 8909 requires spin-offs to be treated, in some ways, as IPOs.

A typical spin-off begins with a public announcement of the parent's intention to divest a subsidiary or division through a pro-rata distribution of new shares to shareholders of record in the parent. It ends perhaps six months later with the distribution of the new shares. Prior to the distribution, management often seeks either an Internal Revenue Service (IRS) ruling or a professional legal opinion on the tax status of the spin-off. The appropriate filings and public disclosure are then provided. Management also seeks shareholder approval when necessary. The size of the subsidiary (measured as a percentage of the entire entity) and the parent's corporate bylaws determine whether shareholder approval is required to carry out the spin-off.

Around the time Form 10 is filed with the SEC, applications are made for exchange listing. The parent may either list the spin-off on an exchange or provide for trading over the counter. Trading in the shares often begins before the actual distribution on a when-issued basis. This trading is often motivated by institutional shareholders who either cannot or do not wish to hold shares in the spin-off company. Initial pricing for the spin-off's shares is determined in the marketplace. Typically, spin-offs trade at rather large bid-ask spreads as market makers and investors seek to establish a value for the spin-offs. A typical disclaimer by the parent as to the listing and valuation of the subsidiary's shares is found in the prospectus filed by Standex International in conjunction with its spin-off of Bingo King:

> The Company has been a wholly-owned subsidiary of Standex since 1971 and, as a result, there has been no public market for Company Common Stock. No assurance can be given that any active market in Company Common Stock will develop after the Spin-off. Bingo King does not presently intend to apply for listing of the Company Common Stock on a stock exchange. Consequently, trading in Company Common Stock, including "when-issued" trading prior to the Spin-off, will occur in the over-the-counter market. The Company Common Stock has been authorized for quotation on the National Association of Securities Dealers Automated Quotations (NASDAQ) system under the NASDAQ symbol: "BNGO". Based upon the number of shares of Standex Common Stock outstanding on the Record Date, a maximum of 1,360,068 shares of Company Common Stock will be distributed in the Spin-off.

Motivations for Spin-Offs

Although spin-offs have been used to split up companies for some time (Section 355 was written in 1952), their popularity as a restructuring device used to extract maximum value from corporate assets has grown dramatically in the 1990s. In a pure spin-off, the parent firm effectively removes itself from the management and ownership of the subsidiary. These distributions are distinct from other types of stock distributions both in terms of intent and effect. Management frequently provides one or more reasons for the spin-off of a division, and these reasons appear in press releases, the prospectus, or an information statement provided to investors when no prospectus is filed.

For example, in 1986 Kraft made the strategic decision to focus on the food processing area and to exit certain unrelated businesses. As part of this restructuring, the company combined four consumer product divisions—Tupperware, Food Equipment Group, West Bend, and

Ralph Wilson Plastics Company—and distributed shares to stockholders as Premark International, Inc.[2] Likewise, in 1985 General Mills spun off two divisions—Crystal Brands and Kenner Parker Toys—to stockholders. According to a statement issued by General Mills, "As historically demonstrated, the toy and fashion industries are substantially more volatile than the company's other businesses. Because of this volatility, the appropriate market value of the toy and fashion operations is not fully realized with these businesses as part of General Mills."[3]

Management attributed Univar Corporation's spin-off of VWR Corporation to the different strategies required for success in the two businesses:

> A principal purpose of the Distribution Plan is to create independent entities designed to pursue the strategies best suited to their individual markets and goals.[4]

Tandycrafts' 1976 spin-off of Stafford-Lowden, Inc., was brought on by more effective deployment of human capital and executive incentive concerns:

> ...the separation will result in more intensive and specialized management leadership in each of the two corporations, the basis for more clearly-defined executive assignments and a stimulus to their executives to maintain management excellence. In addition, following the separation, each of the corporations will have a better framework for management decisions regarding operations and the employment of capital. Finally, the separation is expected to permit a clearer basis for the identification and evaluation of the business of each of the corporations by the customers, employees, the public and the investment community....[5]

A better match between business and financial strategy was the reason provided for Copperweld Corporation's 1986 spin-off of CSC Industries, Inc.:

> The Distribution...will allow each company to arrange such financing in accordance with the needs and capabilities of the different businesses to be operated by each company.[6]

The reasons management cites may be slanted somewhat to impress regulators or the IRS. This is primarily because "creating shareholder value" does not pass the Section 355 business purpose test. As such, market analysts look for the core reason why a split-up versus spin-off occurs. Some reasons and examples are described below.

Lack of Synergy

Companies often opt for spin-offs when the subsidiaries and the parent lack operating, marketing, or financial synergies.

For example, on March 7, 1996, Manor Care Inc. announced that it would spin off Choice Hotels International, the world's second largest hotel company, and retain its health care division, which operates 197 long-term health care facilities. The primary reason for the spin-off was that the two divisions did not offer mutual operating economies. It was felt that each was large enough to attract capital on its own to finance aggressive expansion plans.

In December 1994, General Mills, the $5 billion prepared food company, announced the spin-off of Darden Restaurants ($3 billion in sales), which consisted primarily of the Red Lobster and Olive Garden restaurant chains. According to the company, the prepared food and restaurant businesses are disparate and have distinct cultures that make synergies elusive.

Deconglomerate

Large conglomerates appear to be a thing of the past, and spin-offs have become a very popular way of reversing conglomeration.

For example, on June 13, 1995, ITT, the $24 billion diversified company, announced that it would break up into three companies: (1) ITT Industries, an $8 billion automotive, defense, and electronics company; (2) ITT Destinations (the New ITT), a $5 billion hotel and gaming company that includes the Sheraton and Caesar's World; and (3) ITT Hartford, an $11 billion insurance company. The purpose was to allow these three very different companies to separately pursue and finance their growth strategies.

In January 1996, Hanson PLC, the $18 billion conglomerate, announced that it would split into four independent companies through a spin-off of its chemicals (Millennium Chemicals), energy, and tobacco (Imperial Tobacco) businesses. The new Hanson retained the building materials and equipment businesses.

Focus on Core Businesses

The parent, sometimes under pressure from investors, feels the need to divest itself of non-core business to focus on its primary business.

Take Anheuser-Busch, for instance, which on July 26, 1995 announced it would spin off its packaged bakery goods division, Campbell Taggart, as Earthgrains Co., to concentrate on its core brewing businesses.

One year earlier, on May 17, 1994, Bally Entertainment, a major U.S. casino operator, announced the spin-off of Bally Health and Fitness, the largest and only commercial operator of fitness centers in the United States, to focus exclusively on its gaming business.

Alternative Business and Financial
Strategies Required for Success

Sometimes the parent and subsidiary are in divergent businesses and require different strategies to be competitive. According to Forbes Tuttle of the *IPO Value Monitor,* "a spin-off creates two companies with two clearly defined strategies—not one company with two strategies that sometimes conflict."

For example, in 1996 Baxter International (BAX) reversed its 1995 merger of American Hospital Supply by spinning off its $5 billion hospital and surgical supply business as Allegiance Healthcare Corp. The motivation for the spin-off was to separate BAX's mature, low-margin, and low-growth hospital and surgical supply business from its higher-growth, higher-margin, and more research and development (R&D)-intensive medical products businesses.

On August 4, 1992, Quaker Oats spun off Fisher Price Toys. The food business tends to be cost controlled, low risk, and not capital intensive. By contrast, the toy business is entrepreneurial, high risk, and capital intensive.

Legal/Regulatory

Another reason for a spin-off is that the subsidiary or parent is subject to regulatory pressures adversely affecting the profitability of the corporate system.

For example, on March 3, 1995, Auto Finance Group announced its intention to spin off 95 percent of its equity interest in Patlex Corporation, a subsidiary with royalty interests in laser technologies. Auto Finance Group had previously agreed to be acquired by KeyCorp, and the spin-off was motivated by banking regulations that prohibited KeyCorp from owning over 4.99 percent of nonfinancial businesses.

Undervalued Assets

Sometimes management believes the market undervalues the combined entity and feels that creating separate firms will enable investors and analysts to apply their diverse areas of expertise and value the assets or profit streams more accurately.

For example, on February 19, 1996, the Dial Corporation, a $3.5 billion conglomerate, announced that it would separate the company into two distinct firms—a consumer products company to retain the Dial name and a services company, Viad Corp. The parent would then comprise four product markets—skin care, laundry, household, and food. The new Viad Corp. had three divisions—airline catering and services, convention services, and leisure and payment services. The intent of the spin-off was to achieve a higher valuation by removing a perceived discount applied to the companies' divergent businesses.

Monetize or Capture Value of a Subsidiary

At other times, management will decide to divest a subsidiary with a capitalization that allows the parent to realize value from the transaction.

For example, on June 6, 1995, W.R. Grace, the world's largest specialty chemical business, with sales in excess of $5 billion, announced its intention to spin off National Medical Care (NMC), a $2 billion health services company that operates 600 kidney dialysis centers worldwide. The spin-off was intended to allow W.R. Grace to focus on its core chemicals business. In addition, as part of the spin-off, NMC paid a special dividend of $1.4 billion to W.R. Grace, which the company intended to use to deleverage its balance sheet.

On March 29, 1995, James River Corp., a $5.5 billion manufacturer of paper and paper products, announced the spin-off of Crown Vintage, its $1 billion office paper subsidiary specializing in paper for business uses such as advertising catalogs, direct mail, and office copy paper. According to the company, the spin-off allows James River to "narrow focus and reduce debt and maximize shareholder value."

Riskiness of the Subsidiary

A company may undertake a spin-off if it believes the subsidiary adds excessive volatility to its operating performance. Cooper Industries, a $5 billion conglomerate with business interests in electrical products and power equipment, tools and hardware, and auto products, announced its intention to spin off Cooper Cameron, a manufacturer and marketer of oil and natural gas equipment, in September 1994. The spin-off was part of a two-year program to reduce the company's exposure to cyclical businesses.

Kimberly Clark, an $8 billion manufacturer of household, personal, and health care products as well as newsprint and specialty papers, announced in May 1995 that it would spin off its $500 million cigarette paper operations. These operations had involved the company in lawsuits seeking to recover smoking-related welfare costs, and management did not want to be known as a tobacco industry supplier.

Tax Avoidance

One popular method of selling a business tax free, the Morris Trust, was eliminated in the 1997 tax legislation. A Morris Trust, which accounted for relatively few spin-offs in recent years, basically provided for tax-free spin-offs of unwanted divisions before an acquisition. While Section 355 does not permit tax-free spin-offs for tax avoidance, clearly some spin-offs are structured to minimize tax payments to the government.

Conflicting Business Interests
of Parent and Subsidiary

The parent and subsidiary may conflict if customers think the subsidiary competes with one of its business divisions. Customers may refuse to do business with the subsidiary.

For example, in 1996, ALCO Standard, the largest independent marketer of office technology systems, spun off Unisource Worldwide, its paper and supply systems distribution company, with ALCO to be renamed IKON Office Solutions. The spin-off was prompted by tensions that mounted between the two entities as IKON's outsourcing business increasingly conflicted with Unisource's printing customers.

Avoid a Takeover

Spin-offs can be employed to avoid a takeover of the parent company. For example, on July 12, 1996, Commercial Intertec, in response to a tender offer from Union Dominion Industries (UDI), announced its intention to spin off its $200 million manufacturer of filtration products, Cuno, Inc. The parent, which makes hydraulic systems and metal buildings, was known as TEC after the spin-off. TEC announced, filed for, and effected the spin-off within two months. The spin-off acted as a poison pill because UDI would have to pay capital gains taxes in a post-spin-off acquisition of Cuno.

Issues in Spin-Offs

Section 355 Requirements

A key issue in the active-conduct-of-business area is the ability to provide five years of financial performance data for the subsidiary. The business purpose test stipulates that a spin-off may not be used to distribute profits or dispose of assets. It must be done for a sound business reason, and enhancing shareholder value does not pass the business purpose test. The criteria are subjective and, as Price Waterhouse LLP Tax Partner Gregory Falk states, "Nobody would stake their first-born on whether a spin-off's business purpose will be considered acceptable."

Separation of Assets

In some cases, the division of assets is relatively straightforward if the subsidiary has operated autonomously from the parent. However, the division of assets becomes more difficult when the parent and subsidiary have shared assets over time. Likewise, intangible assets, such as patents and licenses, that have been shared create particularly difficult asset-division decisions.

Capitalization of the Spin-Off and Liabilities

Spin-offs are often viewed as initially undercapitalized and overleveraged. Such was the case with Imperial Tobacco, a 1996 spin-off of Hansen PLC, which was laden with $1.8 billion in debt. Imperial Tobacco had recently gone through a cost-cutting program and faced a tobacco market in secular decline as well as pending lawsuits. Such a situation does not bode well for a spin-off. "Allocation of debt is really the key issue," says Jack Kelly of the investment banking firm Goldman, Sachs. "You want to make each of these companies in terms of debt structure comparable to other companies in their particular industry so that they're not at any kind of competitive disadvantage." In this spirit, most parent firms seek to capitalize spin-offs so as to receive a desired investment-grade debt rating.

Pensions

Pensions can be a particularly difficult issue for parents in spin-offs. The Pension Benefit Guaranty Corp. (PBGC) has taken a tough stance and applied stricter standards in evaluating pension allocations between parents and spin-offs. For example, in the Anheuser-Busch–Earthgrains spin-off, regulators challenged the 7.5 percent yield for the retired and terminated pension liabilities assigned to the spin-off, even though the rate had previously been approved by the IRS in earlier deals. In the end, the parent retained the Earthgrains pension liabilities.

Chief Executive Officer Selection,
Management Team, and Employees

Karen Wruck of the Harvard Business School notes, "A management team has to understand that the spin-off is an organizational and cultural phenomenon, not purely a financial transaction. If it doesn't, you're going to be dead in the water." Luring good management personnel to the spin-off and, as Wruck puts it, "to the less secure but stimulating motivational environment" can be difficult.

Al Wargo, assistant treasurer of Eastman Chemical, the Eastman Kodak spin-off, provides a similar view: "Sure it's a gamble, and it should be if the entrepreneurial spirit is to be ignited." And he points out that in Eastman's case, "There was a pride among the employees about really wanting this thing to work."

Attracting the right employees and making it work can be difficult if the spin-off lacks the financial resources or capitalization to be competitive or is in a highly competitive industry. The most common method of attracting qualified employees is to revamp the incentive compensation system, particularly through the use of stock options and grants. Adds Wruck, "When you spin off a company, it is an opportunity to learn something about your own operation. And if your best managers want to go with the spin-off, it ought to tell you something."

For example, Imation, the $2.25 billion data storage and imaging spin-off of 3M, sought a special type of employee in its 1996 spin-off. Says Chief Financial Officer (CFO) Jill Burchill, "They are the independent thinkers, who like to think outside of the box; they are flocking their way to us." As a lure, Imation developed a broad incentive program tying stock rewards closely to the work that employees actually perform. For example, Burchill helped design a system that links bonus pay and 401(k) contributions to "economic profit" or economic value added (EVA™), as proposed by the consulting firm Stern Stewart. Imation is intent on having its employees understand the importance of providing a return to its shareholders. The employees also will benefit, because they will own about 5 percent of the 42 million shares outstanding.

Contingent Liabilities

Contingent liabilities must be accounted for at the time of a spin-off. Otherwise, down the road management may face a lawsuit for damages from customers or shareholders of either the parent or former subsidiary who believe that the spin-off reduced the ability of the other party to meet uncertain obligations. In a number of cases, parent or subsidiary shareholders have initiated lawsuits years after a spin-off. These lawsuits followed serious downturns in business performance caused by economic conditions, deregulation, or a contingent liability like asbestos.

Corporate Governance and the Board of Directors

In most spin-offs, an internal acting "board of directors" from the parent and soon-to-be-spun-off subsidiary is appointed early in the process. This group performs normal board duties, including the selection of the chief executive officer (CEO) and management team, and legal, regulatory, and accounting preparation for the spin-off. An official board of directors is formally appointed as of the spin-off date. This board usually consists of senior management of the spin-off as well as some members of the parent board who move to the spin-off board. Additional board members are often added through normal shareholder voting procedures in the year or two after the spin-off.

Customer and Shareholder Relations

Good customer and shareholder relations are essential for a spin-off. Post-spin-off, with no parent to rely on, customers are the lifeblood of the new company. In many cases, spun-off companies have found that customers do not understand the spin-off concept and believe that the company is experiencing financial difficulties. Thus, key customers must be kept up to date about the process.

Shareholder relations are also extremely important. As of the ex-date of the spin-off, the shareholders of the parent and spin-off are identical. However, share turnover tends to be rather high soon thereafter. A short-term decline in share price is common soon after a spin-off. Many individual shareholders, who often receive shares in odd lots, simply sell. Institutional shareholders also may sell because the new company is not in a particular index, e.g., the Standard & Poor's (S&P) 500, or is in an industry or size group that is not appealing. Short-term selling may be exacerbated by the fact that spin-offs initially receive very little analyst coverage. As such, good shareholder relations are essential in the early stages.

Spin-Off Do's and Don'ts

As spin-offs have proliferated in the 1990s, many lessons have been learned about their do's and don'ts. This section provides some observations from managers involved in spin-offs.

Why Spin-Offs Make Sense[7]

According to a recent *Wall Street Journal* column, chairman of Premark International Warren Batts "is to corporate spin-offs what Astaire was to the ballroom." As an executive and board member, he has been involved in numerous well-known spin-offs, including Premark–Tupperware, Sears–Allstate/Dean Witter/Discover, and Cooper Industries–Cooper Cameron–Gardner Denver. His assessment as to why spin-offs make sense is rather straightforward:

- The closer managers are to the operating level, the more they focus on the pragmatic details that count.

- Businesses that are ignored by the home office suffer, in part because they have a hard time recruiting and motivating.

- It is hard for a remote part of a big organization to get a hearing, much less execute a turnaround—the brass may be too unfamiliar with it.

From Spin-Off to Success

Kevin Ryan is CEO of Wesley Jessen VisionCare. He arrived at the contact lens maker just as the company was being spun off. He found an organization with demoralized management that had lost its generous benefits, corporate support, and lavish capital budgets. In addition, lax management had led to distribution and production inefficiencies. He realized that the company's strategy and operating philosophy had to change quickly for the company to make it. His six recommendations for successful spin-off management include some very basic principles:

1. *Understand who you really are.* In a futile attempt to compete with the contact lens market leader, the company had failed

to capitalize on its competitive strengths in specialty product niches, where it had patent protection, broad distribution, and consumer franchises. By channeling resources into these areas and extending with product lines, the company successfully expanded (with little capital investment) through opportunities that were always there.

2. *Identify committed managers, guide them in setting goals, and let them run.* Although many people left after the spin-off (and were not enticed to stay), those who remained were committed to making the company successful. These people knew their future depended on their performance and rose to the occasion.

3. *Gear operations to real demand and not wishful thinking.* In an attempt to meet the parent's revenue expectations, previous management had pushed lenses on wholesalers at quarter-end, leading to bloated inventories, numerous returns, and hidden costs. Using the motto "Lenses on eyeballs," the company redirected its efforts toward dispensing lenses to patients and not just stocking the shelves of distributors and eye doctors.

4. *Spend like a start-up.* For a small company, cash is king. Without the parent's checkbook, the spin-off had to cut unnecessary spending to become lean.

5. *"Fire" the unproductive customer.* The old sales-at-any-cost strategy had led to many unprofitable customers. The new approach was to make sure that customers paid a fair price and paid on time.

6. *Reward to the lowest level.* Performance-driven incentives were established for all employees to provide a sense of ownership.

Ryan's observations on the management factors in a spin-off success are mirrored by Wruck of the Harvard Business School: "The ones that tend to be successful are those that have strong management teams and understand that adapting to life as a freestanding company requires them basically to break out of the box, and adopt a new, more entrepreneurial set of management practices."

The Right Spin on Spin-Offs[8]

The Zeneca Group, a pharmaceutical company, was spun off from Imperial Chemicals on June 1, 1993. Within three years, Zeneca's stock price nearly tripled from $29 to $81. As finance director of Zeneca, John Mayo offers some do's and don'ts for spin-offs:

1. Make sure the spin-off does not destroy a core competency. Breaking up businesses that share a technology base or a common R&D process could be lethal.

2. Breaking up businesses that share marketing channels could prove costly.

3. Determine the best financial structure for each business. Consider what each needs to compete in its industry. For example, does one business require a different debt-to-equity ratio than another?

4. Conduct an external test: Are the parts of a company valued differently by shareholders than is the whole?

Recommendations for a Better Deal[9]

In a recent *CFO* magazine article on spin-off problems, the senior executives interviewed came up with six ways to a better deal:

1. *Compose a brief mission statement.* Western Atlas CFO Joseph Casey claims that you must explain your role to the world. Says Casey, "Whether the spin-off is the right thing to do or the wrong thing to do, it will be determined by your customers and shareholders. The worst thing you can have is uncertainty."

2. *Consider having a Wall Street banker.* Harris Computer Systems CEO E. Courtney Siegel says that he decided to use a regional investment banker based on poor acquisition advice—"the worst decision I've made in my professional career."

3. *Search for global efficiencies.* Eastman Chemical found that centralizing such activities as cash management and pension funds created large efficiencies.

4. *Protect against problems during the spin-off.* Tom Oviatt, then executive vice president and treasurer of Ralcorp, encountered staffing, payroll, and tax problems, issues that management should address in any spin-off.

5. *Tune in to other spin-off experiences.* Host Marriott CFO Robert Parsons drew on his firm's experience in separating from Marriott International when Host Marriott Services Corp. was spun off. In particular, a bondholder lawsuit held up the initial spin-off. In the second spin-off, says Parsons, "We set up our financing differently—tying it to the business units. Instead of doing one bond financing for the whole company, we did two: one for the real estate, and one for the airport operations."

6. *Avoid a springtime spin-off.* Helen Cornell, vice president and treasurer of Gardner Denver Machinery Inc., suggests timing the spin-off to avoid the spring. She says, "The big uncertainty is getting through the SEC. Cooper filed the Form 10 at the same time many companies were filing their calendar-year-end proxies. It slowed things down quite a bit."

Previous Spin-Off Research

Several theoretical studies relating to spin-offs (Black and Scholes, 1974, Galai and Masulis, 1976) are grounded in the expropriation hypothesis: Spin-offs are a way for stockholders to transfer wealth away from bondholders. Other studies, however, indicate that spin-offs may be valuable for different reasons. Hakansson (1982) contends that spin-offs may increase the number of portfolio opportunities for stockholders. More recently, Aron (1991) evaluates spin-offs in a principal/agent framework. Her model indicates that spin-offs should enhance operating performance through better incentives and monitoring of management, resulting in higher levels of investment as management appeals to the market to fund projects. This may lead to subsequent merger/takeover activity so that the spin-off can again benefit from the economies of scale as a subsidiary.

Aron (1991) presumes that managers in corporations do not always make decisions in the best interests of shareholders. Therefore, the spin-off process is a good way to monitor managers both before and after the company is actually spun off. An anticipated spin-off gives divisional managers the incentive to increase firm value, which will directly affect their compensation if the transaction takes place. Once the spin-off takes place, the absence of the parent firm means shareholders can monitor managers much more easily. And managers under this type of scrutiny are far more likely to preserve shareholder interests.

Aron also posits a considerable investment upswing just after the spin-off, because the announcement period is typically marked by a stock price increase. The return during this period is a good yardstick for how many positive net present value projects are available to the subsidiary. The spin-off may allow the subsidiary to participate in projects that otherwise would not be possible. Therefore, it is reasonable to expect an increase in R&D spending, capital expenditures or both after the spin-off is complete.

Finally, Aron describes the role of spin-offs in the market for corporate control. After investment in available projects is exhausted, it is efficient for spin-offs to be merged or taken over. The spun-off company may have greatly benefited from the economies of scale afforded it as a subsidiary. Although the spin-off may have been intended to create value, at some point afterwards, a reacquisition may be beneficial.

Empirical studies by Miles and Rosenfeld (1983), Schipper and Smith (1983), and Hite and Owers (1983) demonstrate significantly positive event-day returns associated with the parent firm's announcement of a spin-off. They attribute investors' positive response to parent restructuring and find no evidence supporting the expropriation hypothesis. Cusatis, Miles, and Woolridge (1993) evaluate the value created by spin-offs by examining matched-firm-adjusted stock returns (MFARs) for both parents and spin-offs for up to three years following the spin-off. They find that both parents and spin-offs provide positive abnormal post-spin-off returns, primarily because of corporate restructuring activity. Both spin-offs and their parents experience significantly more takeover activity than do control groups of similar firms. The premiums associated with these takeovers explain most of the abnormal returns. The authors conclude that spin-offs, by dividing a company into separate businesses and thereby effectively creating pure plays for prospective bidders, create value by providing a relatively low-cost method of transferring control of corporate assets to acquiring firms.

Like our present study, a number of recent studies have evaluated accounting performance associated with corporate restructurings. Accounting numbers are used to gauge the effect of changes in corporate form on efficiency, managerial/employee incentives, and agency costs. Although these studies focus on management buyouts (MBOs) rather than spin-offs, they do establish a framework for examining operating performance. DeAngelo (1986) analyzes accounting numbers to determine whether managers tend to understate earnings figures pending an MBO. His results give no indication that management systematically understates earnings.

Kaplan (1989) and Opler (1992) study the performance of MBOs in the years following the buyout. To test the hypothesis that MBOs provide improved incentives, Kaplan looks at changes in (1) operating income before depreciation, (2) capital expenditures, and (3) net operating cash flow. Over the three years following the MBO, the sample experiences an increase in net operating cash flow and a decrease in capital expenditures. His results imply that MBOs provide operating efficiencies and are not merely a wealth transfer. Opler finds similar results for a sample of 44 MBOs completed in the last half of the 1980s.

Smith (1990) further examines post-MBO accounting performance to test whether observed increases in operating performance are the result of changes in accounting procedures or greater efficiency. Included in this study are measures of the management of working capital as well as changes in capital expenditures, such as advertising, maintenance and repairs, and R&D. The results indicate that increased operating performance stems from more efficiently managed working capital after an MBO, rather than decreases in expenditures.

Muscarella and Vetsuypens (1990) test for changes in efficiency to reverse leveraged buyouts (LBOs), or firms that go public after being taken private through an LBO. They examine accounting data for a sample of 72 reverse LBOs by looking for changes in sales, gross margin, operating margin, net margin, asset turnover, and sales per employee. Their results indicate that reorganization via an LBO can lead to better use of resources through decreased agency and operating costs.

2

Spin-Off Operating and Stock Performance

Operating Results

Arguably, a subsidiary that separates from its parent gains from isolating its assets.[10] That is, spin-offs are a subsidiary's escape from bureaucracy and, as such, should reduce agency and overhead costs and thereby enhance operating efficiency. As Forbes Tuttle of the *IPO Value Monitor* says, "It sounds unreal, but it's almost impossible for spin-offs not to work. They force efficiency on companies."

In a large corporation, management accountability may also be limited and investors can lack the information necessary to determine where capital is allocated. Capital allocation for spin-offs is performed by the market rather than by executive fiat. In addition, conglomerates face pressure to pay executives of similar rank comparable amounts, even if they are in different industries. Spin-offs are a means of restoring compensation flexibility. These factors suggest that, over longer periods, the operating performance of spin-offs should improve, leading to higher levels of valuation.

We examined growth rates for several accounting variables to determine the effect of spin-offs on the operating performance of divested subsidiaries. We compiled our data from annual reports as well as from the *Compustat II* database, collecting annual entries for the net sales, operating income (before depreciation), total assets, and capital expenditures.

Investment activity and operating performance data are evaluated from three years before the spin-off (year −3) to three years after the spin-off (year +3). Percentage changes in these accounting variables are measured for five different time intervals covering the pre- and post-distribution period. Year 0 is the year of the spin-off and often reflects performance for less than a full calendar year. Year −1 is thus the most important predistribution year because it provides the most recent report of the accounting variables before the spin-off. The number of firms in our sample for the years before −1 drops considerably because data were unavailable. The numbers decline in year +3 because of mergers, takeovers, and firms dropped for lack of data. Therefore, we focus on the changes that occur between years −1 to +2 and −1 to +3. Most firms report sales and total assets in the time periods before the spin-off. Capital expenditures and operating income are more difficult to locate because of differences in accounting procedures among firms and sporadic reporting in the data sources. Years –1 to +2 have the largest number of observations and closely represent the original sample of 146 spin-offs. Compared with earlier studies that examine restructuring using accounting numbers, the sample in this study is quite large.

To adjust for contemporaneous changes in the market, we formed an industry peer group for each observation. The industry peer group consists of all companies on *Compustat II* within the same two-digit Standard Industrial Code (SIC) industry and over the same period. The change in each company variable is adjusted by the corresponding median change for the industry over the same period. Standard statistical tests are performed on the industry-adjusted medians.

Panel A of table 1 shows the median percentage changes in net sales over different intervals. Net sales grow by 23.0%, 37.1%, and 54.9% for years –1 to +1, –1 to +2, and –1 to +3, respectively. On an industry-adjusted basis, the median percentage changes for the same periods are 5.7%, 2.4%, and 15.3%, respectively. These numbers, shown in figure 1, indicate a gradual but significant increase in sales, with the best performance coming three years following the spin-off.

Panel B of table 1 reports the change in net sales divided by year +1 total assets. Net sales is divided by year +1 total assets for two reasons: (1) to standardize the sales to eliminate the effects of firm size and (2) to better measure efficiency or how much revenue is generated per dollar investment in assets. To remove the confounding effect of increased investment, sales are standardized by first-year total assets. The results in panel B indicate a significant increase in net sales over total assets on both a raw and industry-adjusted basis in all periods following the spin-off.

Table 2 and figure 2 show changes in operating income before depreciation for alternative time intervals. Operating income is used as a measure of operating performance and is reported on a raw and industry-adjusted basis and standardized by year $t+1$ assets. In the years before the spin-off, changes in operating income on an industry-adjusted basis are insignificant. Post-spin-off operating income increases by 35.2%, 42.8%, and 72.1% between years –1 to +1, –1 to +2, and –1 to +3, respectively, which translates into changes of 8.7%, 15.5%, and 23.7% on an industry-adjusted basis over the same periods. These re-

Table 1
Long-Term Operating Performance of Spin-Offs

Summary statistics for changes in net sales and net sales/first-year total assets on a raw and industry-adjusted basis for spin-offs, 1965–91.

Variable	Years Relative to Spin-Off's First Trade				
	−3 to −1	−2 to −1	−1 to +1	−1 to +2	−1 to +3
Panel A: Net Sales					
Median percentage change	21.88%	7.36%	23.03%	37.08%	54.89%
Median industry-adjusted percentage change	5.31%	−0.14%	5.70%	2.37%	15.25%
Z-statistic	1.98**	0.63	1.59	1.60	2.53**
N	84	94	107	89	69
Panel B: Net Sales/First-Year Total Assets					
Median percentage change	22.98%	10.00%	26.82%	40.83%	74.49%
Median industry-adjusted percentage change	1.81%	−0.39%	5.40%	12.88%	23.20%
Z-statistic	1.09	0.80	2.07**	1.71*	2.43**
N	48	74	103	85	65

Note: The z-statistics are based on Wilcoxon signed-rank tests and test the hypothesis that the median industry-adjusted percentage change is equal to zero: The * denotes significance at the .10 level and ** denotes significance at the .05 level.

sults indicate flat performance before the spin-off, followed by an increase in operating income afterwards.

We evaluated two measures of spin-off investment activity—the growth rates in total assets and capital expenditures—over alternative pre- and post-spin-off time intervals. Total assets encompass all investment activity; these are reported by virtually all publicly traded companies and are standard across companies. Panel A of table 3 and figure 3 summarize the results of changes in total assets. Before the spin-off (years −3 to −1), investment activity changes very little and the industry-adjusted figures are not significantly different from zero. Significant growth in total investment does occur in the post-spin-off years. For years −1 to +1, −1 to +2, and −1 to +3, the median change in compa-

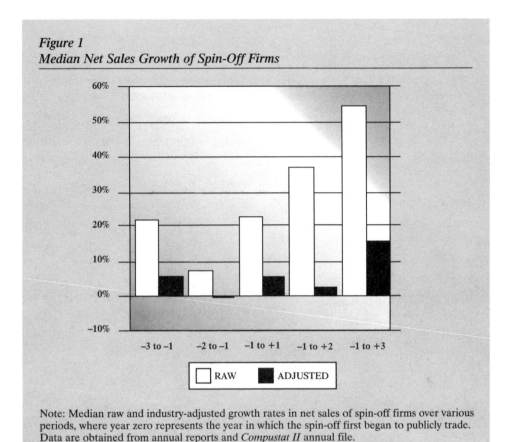

Figure 1
Median Net Sales Growth of Spin-Off Firms

Note: Median raw and industry-adjusted growth rates in net sales of spin-off firms over various periods, where year zero represents the year in which the spin-off first began to publicly trade. Data are obtained from annual reports and *Compustat II* annual file.

nies' total assets on a raw/industry-adjusted basis is 23.0%/7.1%; 40.4%/13.5%; and 52.6%/19.5%, respectively.

Capital expenditures measure the net change in plant, property, and equipment or fixed investment in any given year. Panel B of table 3 and figure 4 show that, on an industry-adjusted basis, changes in capital expenditures for spin-offs were negative but not significantly different from zero. A significant increase in capital investment occurs after the spin-off, especially after several years. As shown in table 3, the median industry-adjusted change in capital expenditures for years −1 to +1, −1 to +2, −1 to +3, on an adjusted basis are 7.9%, 1.1%, and 39.0%, respectively.

Table 2
Long-Term Operating Performance of Spin-Offs

Summary statistics for changes in operating income before depreciation, operating income/sales, and operating income/first-year total assets on a raw and industry-adjusted basis for spin-offs, 1965–91.

		Years Relative to Spin-Off's First Trade			
Variable	−3 to −1	−2 to −1	−1 to +1	−1 to +2	−1 to +3
Panel A: Operating Income Before Depreciation					
Median percentage change	22.36%	17.00%	35.16%	42.80%	72.09%
Median industry-adjusted percentage change	0.86%	8.11%	8.71%	15.47%	23.70%
Z-statistic	1.40	1.11	2.32**	2.47**	1.93*
N	52	75	87	67	55
Panel B: Operating Income/Sales					
Median percentage change	−10.30%	−2.25%	2.61%	0.44%	−0.55%
Median industry-adjusted percentage change	−6.81%	2.56%	4.29%	5.40%	3.63%
Z-statistic	−0.27	0.51	1.94**	1.95**	1.48
N	52	75	87	67	54
Panel C: Operating Income/First-Year Total Assets					
Median percentage change	3.27%	2.03%	4.62%	4.55%	3.58%
Median industry-adjusted percentage change	−0.92%	1.35%	0.64%	0.84%	2.50%
Z-statistic	0.11	2.29**	1.05	0.87	1.36
N	32	70	101	82	63

Note: The z-statistics are based on Wilcoxon signed-rank tests and test the hypothesis that the median industry-adjusted percentage change is equal to zero: The * denotes significance at the .10 level and ** denotes significance at the .05 level.

These results provide evidence that spin-offs spur increased investment activity. Whereas the dollar amount of capital expenditures grows very little in the years before the spin-off, a significant increase in capi-

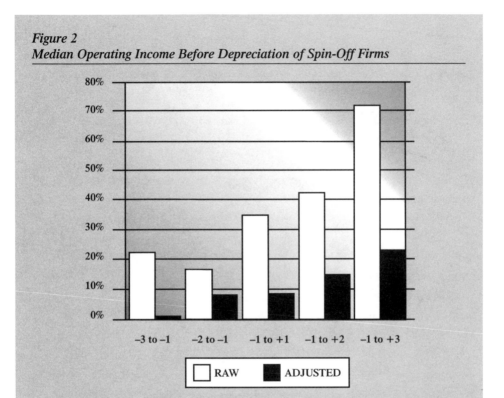

Figure 2
Median Operating Income Before Depreciation of Spin-Off Firms

Note: Median raw and industry-adjusted growth rates in operating income before depreciation of spin-off firms over various time periods, where year zero represents the year in which the spin-off first began to publicly trade. Data are obtained from annual reports and *Compustat II* annual file.

tal expenditures occurs afterwards. These results correspond to and are consistent with the total assets results and indicate that spin-offs generate greater investment activity.

Stock Market Results

The notion of stock market efficiency implies that spin-offs should not offer abnormal performance. In other words, spin-offs should offer a return commensurate with their level of risk. However, certain factors unique to these companies create the potential for mispricing and abnormal stock performance.

Table 3
Long-Term Operating Performance of Spin-Offs

Summary statistics for changes in investment activity, total assets, and capital
expenditures on a raw and industry-adjusted basis for spin-offs, 1965–91.

		Years Relative to Spin-Off's First Trade			
Variable	−3 to −1	−2 to −1	−1 to +1	−1 to +2	−1 to +3
Panel A: Total Assets					
Median percentage change	17.83%	5.43%	23.04%	40.41%	52.64%
Median industry-adjusted percentage change	−2.76%	0.50%	7.11%	13.50%	19.53%
Z-statistic	0.47	0.55	2.57**	2.52**	3.25***
N	49	74	103	85	65
Panel B: Capital Expenditures					
Median percentage change	10.14%	−0.15%	3.92%	9.11%	60.94%
Median industry-adjusted percentage change	−8.55%	−4.79%	7.87%	1.05%	38.97%
Z-statistic	−0.01	0.38	1.73*	1.44	2.16**
N	58	71	83	67	53

Note: The z-statistics are based on Wilcoxon signed-rank tests and test the hypothesis that the
median industry-adjusted percentage change is equal to zero: * denotes significance at the .10
level, ** denotes significance at the .05 level, and *** denotes significance at the .01 level, two-
tailed tests.

In the short term, the uncertainty associated with estimating the intrinsic value of spin-offs may create price volatility. In addition, early
selling pressure can come from investors whose investment universe is
constrained by specific rules and regulations. Many institutional investors are required to invest only in firms with an established record of
paying dividends and must sell their pro-rata shares in spin-offs because
these companies have no history of paying dividends. As the spin-offs
establish a dividend record, more investors are able to hold their shares,
potentially leading to positive abnormal performance. Index funds must
sell shares of firms that are not included in a specific index, such as the

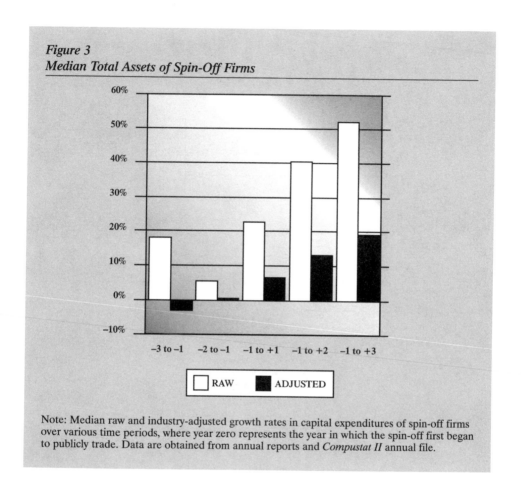

Figure 3
Median Total Assets of Spin-Off Firms

Note: Median raw and industry-adjusted growth rates in capital expenditures of spin-off firms over various time periods, where year zero represents the year in which the spin-off first began to publicly trade. Data are obtained from annual reports and *Compustat II* annual file.

S&P 500. Hence, when an S&P 500 company distributes shares of a subsidiary, index funds must sell the spin-off.

Another factor adding to early selling pressure is that the parent must pay fractional shares in cash.[11] This cash is obtained by withholding shares from the distribution and selling them after a market has developed for the spin-off. The information gap may also contribute to initial selling pressure. Typically, little information is available on spin-offs because they are not initially covered by investor information services and securities analysts. This gap may cause some investors to sell their shares immediately.

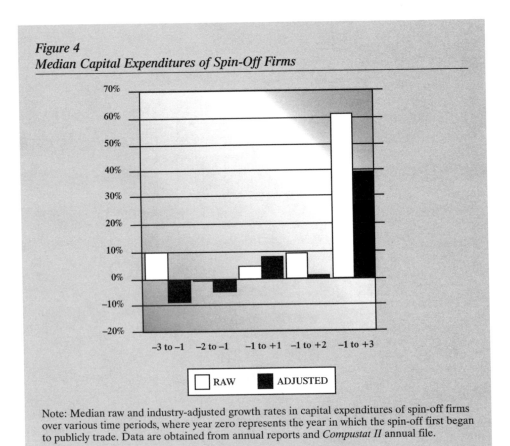

Figure 4
Median Capital Expenditures of Spin-Off Firms

Note: Median raw and industry-adjusted growth rates in capital expenditures of spin-off firms over various time periods, where year zero represents the year in which the spin-off first began to publicly trade. Data are obtained from annual reports and *Compustat II* annual file.

Investors not facing constraints can buy the shares if even the smallest price concession appears. These investors will buy with the intent of reselling the shares at a price that allows expected positive abnormal returns at a later date. Either insufficient capital or insufficient diversification could prevent investors from fully arbitraging this excess-return opportunity.

Over longer periods, the operating performance of the spin-off determines its market value. When spin-offs are distributed to shareholders, the financial results provided in Form S-1 reflect its operating performance as a subsidiary of the parent company. As discussed above, the spin-off's operating performance may improve for a number of reasons. Such improvement would be reflected in future stock prices.

Another source of abnormal returns for spin-offs is the potential for takeover by another firm, which may place a higher value on the spin-off because of perceived operating or financial synergies. Given that improvements in operating performance or takeover offers are not foreseen by the market, possibly because of insufficient information at the time of the spin-off, these factors will not be reflected in initial prices and will produce positive abnormal returns.

Most of the early studies of spin-offs focused on measuring abnormal stock returns at the time of the spin-off announcement.[12] These studies covering the period from the late 1960s through the early 1980s all report mean abnormal returns for spin-offs of about 3 percent. Using our expanded sample of 199 spin-offs, which covers the period from 1965 through 1996, we observe a two-day announcement period abnormal return of 2.9 percent, which is highly significant statistically but somewhat smaller than the earlier estimates. Information pertaining to possible spin-offs is often made available to investors prior to the official announcement, so the two-day announcement effect will not capture the full valuation consequences of spin-offs.

One earlier study reports an abnormal return of more than 20 percent beginning six months before the spin-off announcement through the announcement date. In our study, parent-firm shares exhibit a positive 6.4 percent abnormal return from six months before the distribution date through the distribution date. This 6.4 percent excludes any of the price run-up that might occur earlier. Nevertheless, the market values of the parent firms increase significantly as a result of the spin-off announcement.

We evaluate the stock-return performance for our expanded sample of spin-offs and parents for periods ranging from six months to three years following the spin-off. Spin-off and parent performance are analyzed using raw returns and matched-firm-adjusted stock returns (MFARs). SIC codes and market values are used to identify matched firms for both spin-offs and parents. The MFAR procedure accounts for both contemporaneous market returns and risk. We compute returns presuming a buy-and-hold investment strategy to avoid the bias and transactions costs associated with portfolio rebalancing.

Table 4 provides spin-off stock returns for subperiods corresponding to buying at the closing price on the initial day of trading (day I) and holding for periods of 6, 12, 18, 24, and 36 months.[13] The mean raw re-

Table 4
Long-Term Stock Performance of Spin-Offs: Parametric Tests

Common stock returns for 199 spin-offs for the 1965–1996 period; returns are
reported from one month after the initial day of trade (I) to 6, 12, 18, 24, and 36
months.

	Holding Period				
	I-6	I-12	I-18	I-24	I-36
Panel A: Raw Returns[a]					
Mean return	9.2%	19.6%	31.4%	53.8%	73.7%
t-statistic[c]	3.34***	4.26***	4.49***	5.62***	7.12***
N	199	187	167	154	33
Panel B: Matched-Firm-Adjusted Returns (MFARs)[a,b]					
Mean return	2.8%	6.8%	14.6%	24.7%	29.5%
t-statistic[c]	1.78	2.73**	3.56***	4.37***	4.55***
N	199	187	167	154	33

[a]Returns are computed presuming a buy-and-hold investment strategy. If a firm is delisted or
taken over, the longest available return is used to represent the whole period.
[b]MFARs are calculated as the difference between the carve-out raw returns and the matched-
firm raw returns.
[c]The t-statistics test the hypothesis that the mean holding-period returns are equal to zero:
* denotes significance at the 10 percent level, ** denotes significance at the 5 percent level,
and *** denotes significance at the 1 percent level.

turns (MRRs) for months I-12, I-24, and I-36 are 19.6%, 53.8%, and
73.7%, respectively. The mean MFARs for months I-12, I-24, and I-36
are 6.8%, 24.7%, and 29.5%, respectively. The mean MFARs for
months I-24 and I-36 are both significant at the 1 percent level. We
found similar results using mean S&P 500-adjusted returns and mean
National Association of Securities Dealers (NASD)-adjusted returns.
A consistent finding, regardless of the adjustment procedure used, is
exceptionally good performance during the second year (months 12 to
24). Overall, these returns suggest that spin-offs provide superior long-
term returns to investors.

Stock returns for the parent firms are provided in table 5. The sample size for parent firms is only 177 because (1) some parent firms si-
multaneously distribute two subsidiaries and (2) some cease trading

Table 5
Long-Term Parent-Stock Performance of Spin-Offs: Parametric Tests

Common stock returns for 177 parent firms of spin-offs for the 1962–1996 period; returns are reported from the initial month of trade (I) to 6, 12, 18, 24, and 36 months.

	Holding Period				
	I-6	I-12	I-18	I-24	I-36
Panel A: Raw Returns[a]					
Mean return	6.9%	12.7%	18.6%	32.1%	55.4%
t-statistic[c]	1.67*	2.54**	3.12**	4.43***	5.87***
N	177	167	162	157	152
Panel B: Matched-Firm-Adjusted Returns (MFARs)[a,b]					
Mean return	3.5%	5.9%	9.8%	15.9%	19.3%
t-statistic[c]	1.32	1.62	2.11*	2.84**	3.6**
N	177	167	162	157	152

[a]Returns are computed presuming a buy-and-hold investment strategy. If a firm is delisted or taken over, the longest available return is used to represent the whole period.
[b]MFARs are calculated as the difference between the carve-out raw returns and the matched-firm raw returns.
[c]The *t*-statistics test the hypothesis that the mean holding-period returns are equal to zero: * denotes significance at the 10 percent level, ** denotes significance at the 5 percent level, and *** denotes significance at the 1 percent level.

after the spin-off. Parent-firm returns are measured from the month of the spin-off to month I-6, I-12, I-18, I-24, and I-36. The MRRs for I-12, I-24, and I-36 are 12.7%, 32.1%, and 55.4%, respectively, and the mean MFARs are 5.9%, 15.9%, and 19.3%, respectively.

In evaluating post-spin-off investment performance, we observe the disappearance of a substantial number of our sample firms. By the end of the third year, 113 of the spin-offs are no longer trading. From a stock-performance perspective, firms that are dropped by NASDAQ for failure to meet listing criteria are not likely to be good performers. Conversely, firms dropped on account of takeover activity are apt to be strong performers because of the takeover premiums offered. While not shown here, our results indicated that the stocks of 66 spin-offs that were acquired performed better than average, and the stocks of those that remained trading for the full three years performed worse than average.

Our research indicates that both the spin-offs and their parents offer significantly positive abnormal returns for up to three years beyond the date of the spin-off. These abnormal returns are associated with better spin-off operating performance and corporate restructuring activity. Both spin-offs and their parents are involved in an abnormally high incidence of takeover activity. Fully one-third of the spin-off/parent combinations are involved in takeover activity within three years of the spin-off. We conclude that spin-offs, by dividing a company into separate businesses, enhance operating performance (on average) and can also create value by providing a relatively low-cost method of transferring control of corporate assets to acquiring firms.

Endnotes

1. In contrast, a split-off is an arrangement whereby a subsidiary becomes an independent corporation, but the subsidiary's shares are distributed in a manner that allows the parent and old subsidiary to have different ownership structures for common stock.

2. *Wall Street Journal,* September 9, 1986, p. 12.

3. *Wall Street Journal,* October 30, 1985, p. 40, and General Mills Inc., *Annual Report,* p. 16.

4. VWR Corporation, *Prospectus,* January 31, 1986, p. 1.

5. Stafford-Lowden, Inc., *Prospectus,* March 26, 1976, p. 3.

6. Copperweld Corporation, *Information Statement,* November 11, 1986, p. 5.

7. See Roger Lowenstein, "Confession of a Corporate-Spinoff Junkie," *Wall Street Journal,* March 28, 1996, p. C1.

8. See Catherine Lacoursiere, "Spinoffs Start to Sputter," *Treasury and Risk Management Magazine,* January-February 1997, p. 30.

9. See Roy Harris, "In a Spin," *CFO Magazine,* July 1996, p. 22.

10. The potential for increased operating performance as a result of spin-offs is addressed by Glassman (1988).

11. Fractional shares result from the distribution-split factor. For example, a 1-for-10 distribution-split factor means that a stockholder receives 1 share in the spin-off for every 10 shares held in the parent. All shares not held in increments of 10 must be paid in cash.

12. See J. Miles and J. Rosenfeld, "An Empirical Analysis of the Effects of Spinoff Announcements on Shareholder Wealth," *Journal of Finance* 38, 1983. See also K. Schipper and A. Smith, "Effects of Recontracting on Shareholder Wealth: The Case of Voluntary Spinoffs," and G. Hite and J. Owers, "Security Price Reactions Around Corporate Spinoff Announcements." These articles appeared consecutively in the *Journal of Financial Economics* 12, 1983.

13. Short-term spin-off performance was measured for intervals of up to 40 trading days. Although the short-term mean adjusted returns are predominantly negative, none are significantly different from zero at conventional levels.

Equity Carve-Outs

ECOs involve a partial public offering of a wholly owned subsidiary. Unlike spin-offs, ECOs result in a capital infusion because shares in the subsidiary are offered to the public through an IPO. The parent firm usually retains a controlling interest in the subsidiary. Like spin-offs, ECOs have grown significantly during the 1990s as companies have become more focused on creating shareholder value.

Types of ECOs and Ownership, Accounting, and Tax Issues

The amount of stock sold in an ECO, expressed as a percentage of its total market value, determines the ECO type as well as many of the ownership, accounting, and tax issues. Most arguments favor a parent retaining at least 50 percent ownership in the ECO. Retaining control permits operational and financial relationships between the parent and the ECO to continue and allows the parent to control future corporate governance debates. In addition, as discussed below, there are significant tax advantages to retaining at least 80 percent control.

The parent company's post-carve-out ownership percentage and the associated accounting and tax issues can be summarized as follows. If the parent retains at least 80 percent of the ECO, the parent can consolidate the ECO for tax and accounting purposes, deduct 100 percent of the dividends received from the ECO, and spin off the remaining equity tax free in a Section 355 spin-off. If the parent retains more than 50 percent but less than 80 percent, it loses the ability to consolidate for tax purposes (but not for accounting purposes) and loses the tax advantage of a Section 355 spin-off. However, the parent can still deduct 80 percent of the dividends received from the ECO for tax purposes. If the parent retains more than 20 percent but less than 50 percent, the only difference is that the parent must use the equity method for accounting purposes. If the parent retains less than 20 percent, it must use the cost method instead.

The parent's long-term ownership status in an ECO was recently studied by Salomon Brothers, the investment banking firm. The study reported that for the 1983–1995 period, in 56 percent of ECOs, the parent retained its equity ownership position in the carve-out. The parent's equity interest was spun or split off in 29 percent of the cases, and in 15 percent of the ECOs, the parent reacquired the equity sold to the public. These percentages are similar to the ownership status in the sample of ECOs we studied here.

Filing Requirements and IPO Proceeds

A typical ECO begins with a public announcement of the parent's intention to offer securities in a subsidiary or division through an ECO. Since an ECO represents an initial offering of securities, companies must file an S-1 registration statement with the SEC. Registration requires three years of audited income statements, two years of audited balance sheets, and five years of selected historic financial data. The ensuing process—including preparation of financial and registration statements, SEC review, responses, and amendments, and offering marketing—normally takes up to six months. Once the SEC reviews and declares it effective, the offering can be sold. Applications must also be made for exchange listing. The parent may either list the spin-off on an exchange or provide for trading over the counter.

Either the parent or the carve-out (or both) can receive the proceeds from the IPO. The IPO represents a primary offering if the subsidiary sells the shares. Over 70 percent of our sample was handled in this manner. If the parent sells the shares (known as secondary shares), it must recognize the difference between the IPO proceeds and the parent's basis as a gain or loss for tax purposes. Thermo Electron (TE), which has sold equity in more than 20 subsidiaries over the past 15 years, takes this approach as a means of buffering earnings as it invests in new technologies for future ECOs. If the subsidiary sells the shares in the IPO, neither the parent nor the carve-out incurs a tax liability. In many cases when the ECO sells the shares, some of the proceeds are used to repay loans or pay a special dividend to the parent. A relatively small number of ECOs are handled as joint offerings of the parent and subsidiary.

Use of the proceeds can also become an issue in an ECO. Typically, the proceeds are either retained by the parent or the subsidiary or used to repay debts. In our study, we found that 50 percent of the proceeds of primary offerings are used to repay loans to the parent, 30 percent are retained by the ECO, and 20 percent are paid to creditors (repay debt). In secondary offerings, 50 percent are retained by the parent and 50 percent are paid to creditors. Our study and others, as summarized below, show that the initial stock market reaction to an ECO announcement is more favorable if the subsidiary retains the funds.

After the IPO, all transactions between the parent and the subsidiary must be done on an arm's-length basis and disclosed in the registration statement. It is quite common for the parent to continue to perform certain corporate services, such as investor relations, legal and tax services, human resources, data processing, and banking services, on a contractual basis.

ECO Candidates

Successful ECO candidates tend to be subsidiaries with some or all of the following attributes.

Strong Growth Prospects

If a subsidiary is in an industry with better growth prospects than the parent, the subsidiary will likely sell at a higher price/earnings (P/E) multiple once it has been partially carved out of the parent.

Independent Borrowing Capacity

A subsidiary that has achieved the size, asset base, earnings and growth potential, and identity of a company will generate additional financing sources and borrowing capacity once carved out of the parent.

Unique Corporate Culture

Subsidiaries whose corporate culture differs from that of the parent may be good ECO candidates. The process can provide separation from the parent and the managerial freedom for the ECO to compete as an independent entity. Companies requiring entrepreneurial cultures for success can especially benefit from an ECO.

Unique Industry Characteristics

Unique industry characteristics may enable a subsidiary to improve performance through an ECO. Decentralizing management decision making may allow management to respond in a more timely fashion to changes in technology, competition, and regulation.

Management Performance, Retention, and Rewards

Subsidiaries that compete in industries where management retention is an issue and unique reward systems are required can benefit from an ECO. Furthermore, the company's stock price provides a scoreboard to judge management's performance.

Potential Benefits of ECOs

The potential benefits of ECOs include the following:

- *"Pure play" investment opportunity.* Pure plays have been in much demand by investors in recent years. An ECO, especially for a subsidiary that is not involved in the parent's primary business or industry, increases the subsidiary's visibility as well as analyst and investor awareness, thereby enhancing overall enterprise value. Another reason investors like pure plays created by ECOs is that the separation of the parent and subsidiary minimizes cross subsidies and other potentially inefficient uses of capital.

- *Management scorecard and rewards.* Management is evaluated on a daily basis through the company's stock price. This immediate, visible evaluation can boost performance as managers are free to make important, timely strategic decisions, focus on appropriate value drivers, and be rewarded through a "piece of the action."

- *Capital market access.* An ECO typically improves access to capital markets for both the parent and the subsidiary.

The Benefits of ECOs:
The Thermo Electron Model

No company illustrates the benefits of ECOs better than Boston-based Thermo Electron. TE was a $200 million maker of energy and environmental equipment in 1982 when CEO George Hatsopoulos envisioned using ECOs as a means of building and growing high-tech businesses. The purpose of ECOs at TE is twofold: (1) to raise capital for new ventures and (2) to motivate managers to take appropriate risks. Today, TE and its ECOs make everything from power plants to artificial hearts through 22 different companies created by ECOs. TE's ECOs, which trade on the American Stock Exchange, include such diverse businesses as ThermoLase (hair and skin removal), Thermo Fibertek (recycled fiber and de-inking), Thermo Power (propane gas engines), Thermo Instrument (detection devices for air pollution and toxic substances), and Thermedics (explosives detection and biomedical devices).

TE's ECO model involves using the parent firm, through its Coleman Research division, as a technology core from which new products are developed. As a technology application enters the product development stage, TE involves venture capitalists to provide seed capital and market credibility before selling a minority stake to investors through an IPO. TE uses three criteria for an ECO: (1) opportunities for growth, (2) a strong management team, and (3) attractive IPO prices. While TE maintains a majority stake in each company, it hands over day-to-day control to the entrepreneurs behind the new companies, along with the capital from the IPO and plenty of common share options. TE supplies its spin-outs with human resources, banking, legal, tax, and other services for a flat 1 percent of revenues.

The case of Thermedics demonstrates TE strategy. In 1983, TE sold 14 percent of Thermedics for $6 million. The company had no revenues, but it did have a National Institutes of Health (NIH) grant and CEO Victor Poirier to develop a heart-assist pump. By 1989, the heart-assist pump had not received Food and Drug Administration (FDA) approval, but the company had developed profitable new businesses in biomaterials and explosives detection. At this time, Thermedics sold 40 percent of Poirier's heart pump division to investors for $15 million as Thermo Cardiosystems. By 1996, Thermo Cardiosystems had won FDA

approval for the heart pump, developed over 100 patents, and had nearly $100 million in revenues. Its stock price had risen from a split-adjust-
ed price of $2.27 to $41.50.

The operating and stock return results have been amazing. Since
TE initiated its so-called "spin-out" strategy in 1982, the TE portfolio of
companies has produced a compounded growth rate in earnings of
nearly 30 percent per year. The average annual stock return for the
group is in excess of 25 percent.

Previous ECO Research

The published empirical studies on ECOs involve examining parent-
firm stock-price reactions to the announcement of an ECO. In the first
published study of ECOs, Schipper and Smith (1986) compare the
share-price effects of ECO announcements with those of seasoned equity offerings. They find that, on average, parent-firm shareholders experience positive abnormal returns of about 2 percent for the five-day
period surrounding the announcement of the ECO. In our study, we
find a similar positive abnormal return.

In contrast, a large number of studies have discovered that firms announcing seasoned equity offerings experience negative abnormal returns of roughly 3 percent. Thus, ECOs are the only case in which a
public company announcing a stock sale creates a positive, rather than a
negative, share-price effect. One explanation of the negative abnormal
returns normally associated with seasoned equity offerings is that managers holding private information regarding the true value of the parent
assets will announce a seasoned equity offering when the parent stock is
overvalued. Schipper and Smith (1986) hypothesize that separating subsidiary growth opportunities from parent assets, which occurs during an
ECO, avoids such a situation.

Schipper and Smith also find that ECOs appear to be a temporary
arrangement. In their sample of 76 carve-outs during the 1965–1983 period, 48 did not survive in the same parent-subsidiary relationship that
existed immediately after the ECO took place. Of those 48 firms, 26
were taken over, 7 were spun off, and 15 were sold to another firm.

Klein, Rosenfeld, and Beranek (1991) further examine the findings of
Schipper and Smith. They confirm that ECOs appear to be a temporary

arrangement. Forty-two carve-outs in their sample of 52 involve a "second event," defined as one in which the parent firm either (1) reacquires all outstanding shares in the carve-out, creating, once again, a wholly owned subsidiary or (2) sells off all its interest in the carve-out, either to the public or to another firm(s). In either case, the ECO ceases to exist as such.

Klein, Rosenfeld, and Beranek (1991) examine the effects of both the first announcement of an impending ECO and the second announcement that it will no longer exist. They find that the combined parent-firm stock-price response to the announcement of the carve-out and the subsequent event depends on the nature of the second event. If the parent sells off the carve-out, the parent-firm shareholders experience statistically significant positive abnormal returns over each separate announcement period, as well as over both periods combined. On the other hand, if the parent reacquires the carve-out, the parent-firm shareholders experience statistically significant positive abnormal returns over each separate announcement period, but the combined performance measure is not statistically significant. The carve-out stock-price response to announcements of both types of second events is positive. However, gains to subsidiary shareholders on the announcement date are offset by the subsidiary's negative abnormal returns over the trading period preceding the second event.

Agarwal (1994) provides evidence consistent with the existing literature regarding the positive share-price effect for parent firms announcing ECOs. However, he also concludes that carved-out IPOs do not exhibit any underpricing, which is inconsistent with Schipper and Smith (1986). They find a 1.7 percent average initial return for 40 of the ECOs in their sample.

Allen (1993) investigates the determinants of the market response to announcements of ECOs. He finds evidence indicating that parent-firm stock-price returns are highly dependent on the intended use of the IPO proceeds. For his sample of 108 ECOs during the 1978–1991 period, he finds that the average market response is positive only when parent firms receive funds. Gains increase significantly when parent firms pay proceeds to creditors.

Nanda (1991) provides a theoretical background to the existing literature by extending the signaling model developed by Myers and Majluf (1984). He hypothesizes that firms raise capital through ECOs when insiders have information to suggest that subsidiary shares would fetch a value above their true worth. If this were the entire argument, we would predict that ECOs mean wholly owned subsidiaries are over-valued, and parent share prices should fall after ECO announcements. However, ECO announcements also convey information that insiders chose not to issue shares in the parent firm—a signal that might imply undervaluation of parent-firm shares. Thus, Nanda's model implies that large parent firms with relatively small subsidiaries ought to experience share-price increases following ECO announcements.

Slovin, Sushka, and Ferraro (1995) test one aspect of the Nanda model. They infer from his model that a carve-out announcement will signal the bad news that managers view subsidiary assets as overvalued. They hypothesize that, if investors interpret an ECO decision as unfavorable news about the value of subsidiary assets, and if at least a portion of this news applies to firms engaged in similar economic activities, then the share-price effects on rivals of carved-out subsidiaries should be more unfavorable. For the period of the carve-out announcement, they observe statistically significant negative abnormal returns for the firms in the same industry as the carved-out subsidiary. Their sample consists of 36 ECOs over the period 1980–1991.

Jongbloed (1992) asserts that differences in the investment opportunity sets and regulatory environments of parents and subsidiaries lead to costs that can be avoided if they are separated. He compares two methods of subsidiary separation: the spin-off and the ECO. He finds that subsidiaries involved in ECOs have more growth opportunities than their parents, whereas subsidiaries involved in spin-offs have fewer.

Aron (1991) develops a moral hazard argument pertaining to reasons why firms might want to either carve out or spin off a subsidiary. Her model implies that divisions or subsidiaries with many investment opportunities or growth options cannot provide sufficient incentives for division managers by distributing either shares or options on shares of the parent firm. Efficient incentives can be provided only when shares in the much smaller subsidiary or division are publicly traded. Thus, Aron's model implies that spin-offs or ECOs would be followed by heavy investment activity by the divested or carved-out subsidiary.

In many instances, a parent firm will retain a majority stake in its carved-out subsidiary after the ECO. There are two competing hypotheses in the area of equity ownership and its relationship to firm value. The first, the convergence-of-interests hypothesis, predicts that larger management stakes should be associated with higher market valuation of the corporation. Jensen and Meckling (1976) argue that, as management ownership rises, the agency costs associated with the misalignment of management interests declines. In other words, management's interests become more closely aligned with shareholders' interests. Therefore, management will make a more concerted effort to maximize shareholder wealth as its equity ownership in the firm rises.

The second hypothesis, the entrenchment hypothesis, suggests that market valuation can be adversely affected for some range of high management stakes in ownership. Demsetz (1983) and Fama and Jensen (1983) point out that when a manager owns only a small stake in the firm, market discipline may still force him or her to maximize value. However, as the manager's stake rises, he or she may have enough voting power or influence to guarantee employment with the firm at an attractive salary.

Many empirical studies have attempted to test these two competing hypotheses. Most support the convergence-of-interests hypothesis. Demsetz and Lehn (1985) provide an empirical study of the structure of corporate ownership and its relationship to firm value. They argue that the ownership structure varies systematically in ways that maximize value. They find no significant relationship between ownership concentration and accounting profit rates.

Morck, Shleifer, and Vishny (1988) further investigate the relationship between management ownership and firm value, as measured by Tobin's Q. They find evidence of a significant nonmonotonic relationship between the two. They observe that, as the ownership by the board of directors rises, Tobin's Q first increases, then declines, and finally rises slightly. Stulz (1988) also finds a nonmonotonic relationship between management control and firm value. He shows that, if managerial control of voting rights is small (large), shareholders' wealth rises (falls) when management strengthens its control of voting rights.

Holderness and Sheehan (1988) examine the role of majority share-holders in publicly held corporations. They find that when the majority block trade, stock prices increase. They also find that large numbers of firms with majority shareholders are surviving. Thus, their results are inconsistent with the notion that individuals or corporations hold majority blocks of stock in publicly traded corporations primarily to expropriate or consume corporate resources.

Kim, Lee, and Francis (1988) find that corporations with high degrees of insider ownership enjoy superior returns as compared with firms with more diffuse ownership. Hudson, Jahera, and Lloyd (1992) also find a direct, significant relationship between insider ownership and firm performance. McConnell and Servaes (1990) investigate the relationship between Tobin's Q and ownership structure. While Morck, Schliefer, and Vishny (1988) regress Tobin's Q ratios against three different ranges of board ownership (0 to 5 percent, 5 to 25 percent, and over 25 percent) using piecewise linear regressions, McConnell and Servaes (1990) regress Tobin's Q ratios against various measures of ownership, including fractions of shares owned by insiders, individual atomistic shareholders, block shareholders, and institutional investors. McConnell and Servaes observe a significant curvilinear relation between Tobin's Q and the fraction of common stock owned by corporate insiders. The curve slopes upward until insider ownership reaches approximately 40 to 50 percent, and then slopes slightly downward.

One final area of related research involves IPOs. ECOs are actually a specific type of IPO. In an ECO, new shares in a previously wholly owned subsidiary are sold to the public. Ibbotson, Ritter, and others have studied the price performance of IPOs. Most of these studies report similar results: (1) IPOs, on average, are initially underpriced, leading to an average first-day return in the 10 to 15 percent range and (2) IPOs, on average, tend to underperform market indexes and industry peers by 5 to 8 percent per year over their first three years of existence. Underpricing tends to be more pronounced in periods called "hot issue" markets, when many IPOs, typically in similar industries, come to the market. However, the underpricing of IPOs is a short-run phenomenon. Their longer term performance, on average, is decidedly negative relative to the market and peers.

ECO Operating and Stock Performance

Operating Results

Table 6 reports median raw and industry-adjusted rates of change over time for the carve-out accounting variables. Panel A reports growth rates in net sales. All periods involving the ECO year zero and beyond indicate positive, statistically significant growth rates in net sales. For the period (−1 to +1), the growth rate in median net sales is 20.7 percent on an industry-adjusted basis. Sixty-one carve-out firms are represented. Figure 5 depicts the raw and industry-adjusted changes in net sales for carved-out subsidiaries before and after their IPOs.

Panel B of table 6 reports growth rates in operating income before depreciation. Once again, all periods involving the ECO year zero and beyond indicate positive, statistically significant growth rates in income for at least one statistical test. For the period −1 to +1, the growth rate in median operating income before depreciation is 27.8 percent on an industry-adjusted basis. Fifty carve-out firms are represented. Figure 6 depicts the raw and industry-adjusted changes in operating income before depreciation for carved-out subsidiaries before and after their IPOs.

Panels C and D of table 6 report similar findings for carve-out firms' growth rates in total assets and capital expenditures, respectively. The median industry-adjusted growth rate in total assets for the −1 to +1 period is 25.0 percent. The median industry-adjusted growth rate in capital expenditures for the same period is 33.9 percent. Sixty-one carve-out firms are represented in panel C; 42 are represented in panel D. Figures 7 and 8 show the changes in carve-out total assets and carve-out capital expenditures, respectively.

Panels E, F, G, and H of table 6 present various ratios of the above accounting variables for standardization purposes. Panel E reports growth rates in the ratio of net sales divided by total assets. The median industry-adjusted growth rate for years −1 to +1 is 1.4 percent; this figure is not statistically significant. For periods −1 to +2 and −1 to +3, growth rates are negative and statistically significant, perhaps because total assets are growing faster than net sales during this period. Panel F reports growth rates in the ratio of operating income before depreciation divided by net sales. None of these figures is statistically significant.

Table 6
Operating Performance of Carve-Outs: Nonparametric Tests

Growth rate figures for median accounting variables for all available carve-outs on a raw and an industry-adjusted basis.[a]

	Year Relative to Carve-Out's First Trade			
	−2 to -1	−1 to +1	−1 to +2	−1 to +3
Panel A: Net Sales (in $MM)				
Median raw growth rate	11.63%	41.30%	59.33%	86.94%
Median industry-adjusted rate	3.18%	20.66%	29.79%	49.42%
M(sign)[b]	1.5	17.5***	11.5***	10.5***
p-value	(0.5488)	(0.0001)	(0.0018)	(0.0025)
Sgn Rank[c]	17	677.5***	449***	351.5***
p-value	(0.1475)	(0.0001)	(0.0001)	(0.0001)
N	11	61	51	45
Panel B: Operating Income Before Depreciation (in $MM)				
Median raw growth rate	15.57%	52.72%	67.99%	83.96%
Median industry-adjusted rate	−2.11%	27.84%	35.58%	57.50%
M(sign)[b]	0	5	4.5	3
p-value	(1.0000)	(0.2026)	(0.1996)	(0.3915)
Sgn Rank[c]	−3	272.5***	170**	156.5***
p-value	(0.7422)	(0.0072)	(0.0156)	(0.0056)
N	8	50	39	34
Panel C: Total Assets (in $MM)				
Median raw growth rate	24.41%	50.27%	84.26%	137.59%
Median industry-adjusted rate	17.28%	24.98%	48.06%	94.36%
M(sign)[b]	0.5	16.5***	18.5***	14.5***
p-value	(1.0000)	(0.0001)	(0.0001)	(0.0001)
Sgn Rank[c]	15	681.5***	550***	421.5***
p-value	(0.2061)	(0.0001)	(0.0001)	(0.0001)
N	11	61	51	45
Panel D: Capital Expenditures (in $MM)				
Median raw growth rate	52.52%	57.34%	56.77%	73.89%
Median industry-adjusted rate	34.11%	33.92%	55.00%	57.62%
M(sign)[b]	2.5*	5	2.5	6.5**
p-value	(0.0625)	(0.1641)	(0.4996)	(0.0241)
Sgn Rank[c]	7.5*	227.5***	157***	123.5***
p-value	(0.0625)	(0.0032)	(0.0081)	(0.0053)
N	5	42	35	29

Table 6
Operating Performance of Carve-Outs: Nonparametric Tests (Continued)

	Year Relative to Carve-Out's First Trade			
	−2 to −1	−1 to +1	−1 to +2	−1 to +3
Panel E: Net Sales / Total Assets (in $MM)				
Median raw growth rate	−3.38%	−1.15%	−11.44%	−21.11%
Median industry-adjusted rate	−6.60%	1.38%	−7.96%	−14.25%
M(sign)[b]	−0.5	1	−9**	−9***
p-value	(1.0000)	(0.8974)	(0.0153)	(0.0096)
Sgn Rank[c]	−6	−25	−176.5*	−218***
p-value	(0.6377)	(0.8558)	(0.0885)	(0.0093)
N	11	60	50	44
Panel F: Operating Income Before Depreciation/Net Sales (in $MM)				
Median raw growth rate	3.60%	1.07%	−2.95%	−7.58%
Median industry-adjusted rate	1.70%	4.51%	1.66%	−3.03%
M(sign)[b]	0	1	0.5	0
p-value	(1.0000)	(0.8877)	(1.0000)	(1.0000)
Sgn Rank[c]	−3	49.5	12	−35.5
p-value	(0.7422)	(0.6375)	(0.8695)	(0.5518)
N	8	50	39	34
Panel G: Operating Income Before Depreciation/Total Assets (in $MM)				
Median raw growth rate	−5.85%	−10.55%	−16.93%	−21.79%
Median industry-adjusted rate	−3.17%	−1.44%	−12.35%	−13.92%
M(sign)[b]	0	−1	−5.5	−5
p-value	(1.0000)	(0.8877)	(0.1081)	(0.1214)
Sgn Rank[c]	−5	27.5	−16	−69.5
p-value	(0.5469)	(0.7937)	(0.8266)	(0.2403)
N	8	50	39	34
Panel H: Capital Expenditures/Net Sales (in $MM)				
Median raw growth rate	10.27%	1.13%	−18.08%	−5.53%
Median industry-adjusted rate	32.48%	−1.94%	−7.23%	−10.14%
M(sign)[b]	2.5*	−1	−0.5	−1.5
p-value	(0.0625)	(0.8776)	(1.0000)	(0.7111)
Sgn Rank[c]	7.5*	88.5	53	15.5
p-value	(0.0625)	(0.2736)	(0.3931)	(0.7439)
N	5	42	35	29

[a]Data are collected using the *Compustat II* annual file.
[b]The two-tailed sign statistics (M(sign)) test the null hypothesis that the median industry-adjusted rates are equal to zero: * denotes significance at the 10 percent level, ** denotes significance at the 5 percent level, and *** denotes significance at the 1 percent level.
[c]The two-tailed Wilcoxon signed rank statistics (Sgn Rank) test the null hypothesis that the median industry-adjusted rates are equal to zero: * denotes significance at the 10 percent level, ** denotes significance at the 5 percent level, and *** denotes significance at the 1 percent level.

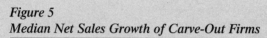

Figure 5
Median Net Sales Growth of Carve-Out Firms

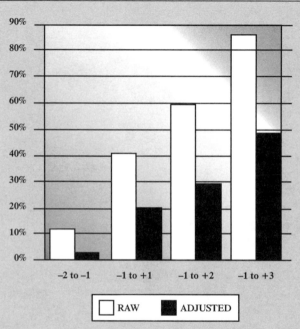

Note: Median raw and industry-adjusted growth rates in net sales of carve-out firms over various time periods, where year zero represents the year in which the carve-out first began to publicly trade. Data are obtained from the *Compustat II* annual file.

The median industry-adjusted growth rate for years –1 to +1 is 4.5 percent. Panel G reports growth rates in the ratio of operating income before depreciation divided by total assets. Again, none of the growth rates are statistically significant. The median industry-adjusted growth rate for years –1 to +1 is –1.4 percent. Panel H reports growth rates in the ratio of capital expenditures divided by net sales. None of these figures are statistically significant. The median industry-adjusted growth rate for years –1 to +1 is –1.9 percent.

Because none of the relative growth rates in panels E, F, G, and H are positive or statistically significant, we cannot conclude that the significant increases in sales, operating income before depreciation, total assets, and capital expenditures documented in panels A, B, C, and D

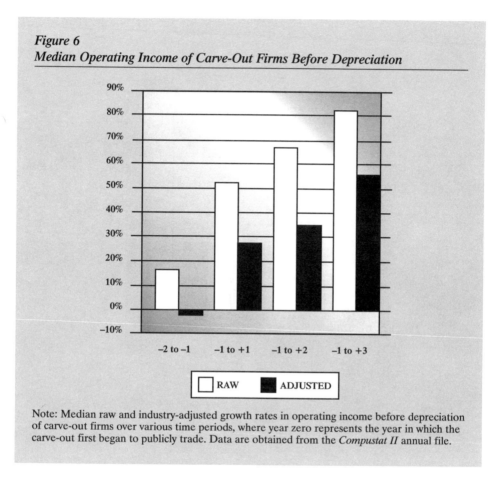

Figure 6
Median Operating Income of Carve-Out Firms Before Depreciation

Note: Median raw and industry-adjusted growth rates in operating income before depreciation of carve-out firms over various time periods, where year zero represents the year in which the carve-out first began to publicly trade. Data are obtained from the *Compustat II* annual file.

are due to increased operational efficiencies alone. Rather, it appears that these increases in operating performance are due in part to an increase in the scale of the carve-out's operations after it goes public.

Stock Market Results

Table 7 shows the results of the average long-term stock market performance of ECOs over various holding periods. Panel A reports the raw returns for carve-out firms, and panel B reports the MFARs for the same carve-out firms. For all holding periods represented, the raw returns are positive and statistically significant. MFARs are also positive, but are statistically significant only for the 36-month holding period.

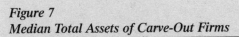

Figure 7
Median Total Assets of Carve-Out Firms

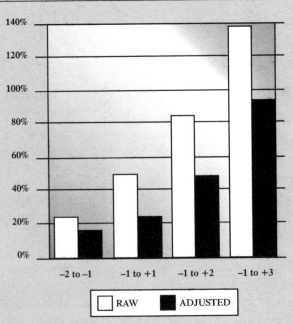

Note: Median raw and industry-adjusted growth rates in total assets of carve-out firms over various time periods, where year zero represents the year in which the carve-out first began to publicly trade. Data are obtained from the *Compustat II* annual file.

Over the 36-month holding period that begins one month after the carve-out starts to publicly trade, carve-out shareholders received average returns of 54.7 percent on a raw basis and 28.7 percent on a matched-firm-adjusted basis. Over the 6-, 12-, 18-, and 24-month holding periods, carve-out shareholders received average MFARs of 5.0 percent, 11.9 percent, 8.2 percent, and 11.8 percent, respectively. The results are similar when returns are adjusted for S&P 500 Index returns.

It should be noted that ECOs, like spin-offs, are subject to much takeover activity. In our sample, 39 of the 87 ECOs are acquired within three years. An analysis of returns indicates that ECOs that are taken over perform better than average, while those that are not taken over

Figure 8
Median Capital Expenditures of Carve-Out Firms

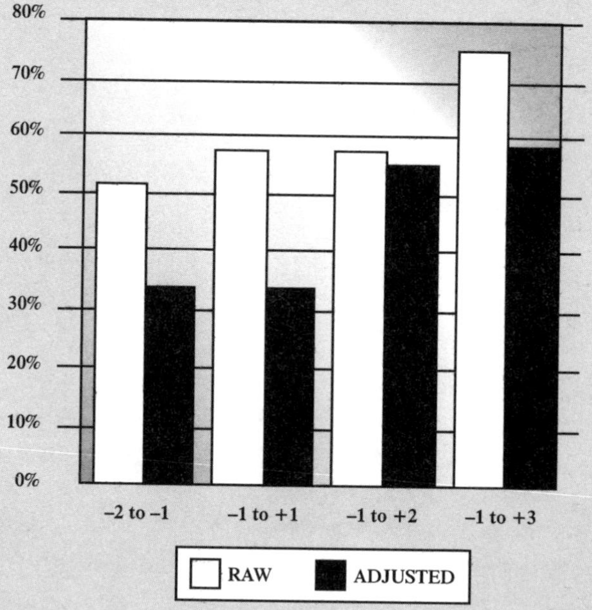

Note: Median raw and industry-adjusted growth rates in capital expenditures of carve-out firms over various time periods, where year zero represents the year in which the carve-out first began to publicly trade. Data are obtained from the *Compustat II* annual file.

perform worse than average. Nonetheless, even the latter outperform, on average, the matched firms.

Overall, these results are inconsistent with Klein et al. (1991) and Ritter (1991), who find that ECOs and IPOs, respectively, generate negative abnormal returns in the long run. Further, these results do not support Nanda's (1991) conjecture that ECOs fetch a price in excess of their true value. If this were the case, then we would not see ECOs outperforming the matched-firm sample in the long run. Our results are more consistent with the hypotheses of Schipper and Smith (1986) and Aron (1991). ECOs may allow for increased operating efficiencies. Our operating performance results are also consistent with that idea.

Table 7
Long-Term Stock Performance of Carve-Outs: Parametric Tests

Common stock returns for 87 ECOs for the 1981–1993 period; returns are reported from one month after the initial day of trade (I) to 6, 12, 18, 24, and 36 months.

	Holding Period				
	I-6	I-12	I-18	I-24	I-36
Panel A: Raw Returns[a]					
Mean return	12.81%	28.97%	29.01%	32.59%	54.65%
t-statistic[c]	2.02**	1.89**	3.20***	3.55***	4.12***
N	87	87	87	87	87
% positive	55%	54%	57%	55%	59%
Panel B: Matched-Firm-Adjusted Returns (MFARs)[a,b]					
Mean return	5.04%	11.89%	8.21%	11.83%	28.65%
t-statistic[c]	0.78	0.73	0.78	1.14	1.99**
N	87	87	87	87	87
% positive	55%	62%	56%	55%	60%

[a]Returns are computed presuming a buy-and-hold investment strategy. If a firm is delisted or taken over, the longest available return is used to represent the whole period.

[b]MFARs are calculated as the difference between the carve-out raw returns and the matched-firm raw returns.

[c]The t-statistics test the hypothesis that the mean holding-period returns are equal to zero: * denotes significance at the 10 percent level, ** denotes significance at the 5 percent level, and *** denotes significance at the 1 percent level.

The results of the stock market performance of parent firms over the long run, as depicted for various periods, are provided in table 8. Panel A reports the raw parent-firm returns, and panel B reports the MFARs for parent firms. Although raw parent-firm returns are positive and sometimes significant for all holding periods represented, MFARs for parent firms are not. Over all holding periods represented, MFARs for parent firms are negative. For the 6-, 18-, and 24-month holding

Table 8
Long-Term Parent-Stock Performance of Carve-Outs: Parametric Tests

Common stock returns for 87 parent firms of ECOs for the 1981-1993 period; returns are reported from the carve-out's initial day of trade (I) to 6, 12, 18, 24, and 36 months.

	Holding Period				
	I-6	I-12	I-18	I-24	I-36
Panel A: Raw Returns[a]					
Mean return	1.33%	6.70%	10.45%	17.60%	36.86%
t-statistic[c]	0.33	1.27	1.84*	2.90***	3.92***
N	87	87	87	87	87
% positive	44%	46%	55%	64%	63%
Panel B: Matched-Firm-Adjusted Returns (MFARs)[a,b]					
Mean return	−8.73%	−5.80%	−12.83%	−12.00%	−10.36%
t-statistic[c]	−1.62*	−0.97	−1.71**	−1.51*	−0.80
N	87	87	87	87	87
% positive	39%	39%	34%	40%	46%

[a]Returns are computed presuming a buy-and-hold investment strategy. If a firm is delisted or taken over, the longest available return is used to represent the whole period.

[b]MFARs are calculated as the difference between the carve-out raw returns and the matched-firm raw returns.

[c]The *t*-statistics test the hypothesis that the mean holding-period returns are equal to zero: * denotes significance at the 10 percent level, ** denotes significance at the 5 percent level, and *** denotes significance at the 1 percent level.

periods, these negative returns are statistically significant. Parent-firm shareholders received an average MFAR of −8.7 percent over 6 months, −5.8 percent over 12 months, −12.8 percent over 18 months, −12.0 percent over 24 months, and −10.4 percent over 36 months after the initial trade of their carved-out subsidiaries. Thus, the long-term performance of parent firms differs dramatically from that of the ECOs.

Summary

Our research indicates that ECOs earn significantly positive abnormal stock returns for up to three years beyond the date of the carve-out. Parents, on the other hand, earn negative stock returns. As with spin-offs, the abnormal stock returns of ECOs are associated with better spin-off operating performance and corporate restructuring activity. We conclude that ECOs appear to be a restructuring device that leads to better operating performance (on average) and greater increases in shareholder value.

AT&T's Spin-Off of Lucent Technologies and NCR

On September 20, 1995, AT&T announced that it would split its operations into three publicly traded companies: (1) AT&T, a communications services firm, (2) a network systems company later named Lucent Technologies, and (3) NCR, a computer business. There were three stages to the AT&T split-up: (1) a sale of about 17 percent of Lucent Technologies to investors through an IPO or ECO, (2) a tax-free spin-off of AT&T's remaining 83 percent in Lucent to AT&T stockholders, and (3) a tax-free spin-off of NCR. The announcement was greeted with enthusiasm by investors, as AT&T's stock closed at $63.75, up $6.125 or 11 percent.

The move was made to eliminate the conflicts caused by deregulation. Network Systems customers were becoming competitors in local and long-distance services. The move also allowed AT&T to focus on its core communications services, which provided 60 percent of its sales and 80 percent of its profits. And AT&T's split-up was not original—ITT Corporation had split into three units nine months before. Nonetheless, the split-up left AT&T as the biggest pure play in communications, with annual revenues of nearly $50 billion.

The two divested companies had diverged in performance in recent years. The Network Systems unit, the world's largest provider of communications equipment such as switches and phone lines, had produced solid financial results for AT&T. But concerns loomed as its biggest customers, the Baby Bells, became reluctant to buy from AT&T, a competitor in cellular markets and a potential competitor in local markets. The computer business, on the other hand, had lost millions of dollars since its purchase in 1991.

In summing up the divestiture, AT&T CEO Robert Allen noted, "The complexity of trying to manage these different businesses began to overwhelm the advantages of our integration. The world has changed.

Markets have changed. Conflicts have arisen, and each of our businesses has to react more quickly." Richard Miller, AT&T's low-profile
CFO, stated the motivation quite succinctly: "Customers were telling us
that we were losing business because there were too many conflicting
parts working against each other."

Background

After the 1984 breakup of AT&T and the Baby Bells, AT&T focused on
long-distance service and communications equipment. Over the next
decade, changes in regulation and advances in technology led to
tremendous growth in the communications services and two divergent
trends for AT&T. Deregulation fostered growth in the demand for long-
distance service; for AT&T this meant more competition and lower
prices and margins. The same deregulation that fostered the growth of
communications services, however, also created higher demand for
communications equipment from AT&T's Network Systems group. To
provide customers with integrated voice and data communications,
AT&T purchased McCaw Cellular and NCR.

Unfortunately, the integration of long-distance and cellular services, combined with Network Systems and the computer business, did
not provide the desired results. Many of the purported synergies never
developed, and each unit was facing competitive pressures: The long-
distance business was competing with MCI, Sprint, and eventually the
Baby Bells; the cellular services were competing with the Baby Bells
and other cellular service providers. The Network Systems business
began to find that the Baby Bells, its biggest customers, were unwilling
to buy from a competitor in cellular markets and eventually in local
markets. Further, computer services were never fully integrated into
communications services.

As a result of the competitive pressures on AT&T's businesses and
the company's inability to achieve desired synergies, AT&T's stock
price languished in the 1990s. Despite the fact that the Dow Jones
Industrial Average more than doubled between 1990 and 1995,
AT&T's stock was still trading in the $50 range as of 1995—the same
price as January 1990. Consequently, AT&T's strategy was criticized
for not producing results. Nonetheless, AT&T's September 20, 1995,

announcement that it was splitting into three separate companies shocked the financial community and its competitors.

The Second Break-Up of AT&T

The split-up, or trivestiture, of AT&T led to three distinctly different companies: AT&T, a communications firm with $49 billion in revenues, consisting of communications services, wireless services, the Universal Credit card, AT&T Solutions, and AT&T Laboratories, had 121,000 employees. Lucent Technologies, a communications systems and equipment company with $21.4 billion in revenues, including business communications systems, consumer products, AT&T Paradyne, and microelectronics, had 131,000 employees. NCR, a computer and information solutions company with $8.2 billion in revenues, focusing on retail, financial, and communications with limited personal computer production, had 41,100 employees.

Motivation

Many market observers believed that AT&T's restructuring decision was motivated in part by the lackluster appreciation of its stock price in recent years. The initial run-up in AT&T's stock price is typical of company split-ups. Many investors like pure plays, companies with focused businesses that let investors do the diversifying. The net result is that the sum of the parts may be worth more than the whole. Likewise, the valuation of the disparate businesses of large companies is a difficult task and is often a concern for analysts and investors. Managers often cite undervaluation as a problem and as a motivation for a split-up. This issue was addressed by AT&T's Allen: "The market value of AT&T was being buried. Investors could not understand the strategy of the combined company."

In the longer run, the split-ups' stocks tend to do quite well. In fact, one need only look to the previous split-up of AT&T to see the stock market benefits. Since the January 1, 1984, breakup of AT&T and the Baby Bells, the market value of all the companies has grown sixfold, compared with a fivefold increase in the S&P 500.

4

When AT&T announced the massive restructuring, analysts reacted favorably and cheered Allen for the bold move. Mario Gabelli, who heads Gabelli Asset Management and is a frequent management critic, stated, "The strategy that Robert Allen is following is very, very sound, very, very smart."

Analysts expected four benefits from the split-up: (1) The management of each company could now focus on their specific markets; (2) the equipment company would not lose the Baby Bells' business because of its association with the service company; (3) the service company would be free to compete without concerns about offending equipment buyers; and (4) the computer company could make a go of it on its own, without draining cash from the other companies.

Time Line

Planning for the split-up of AT&T began in spring 1995 under the code name project NOVA. Working with AT&T's long-time investment banker, Morgan Stanley, senior management devised the strategy and initiated the process for the second split of AT&T in 11 years. The details of the strategy and the related agreements and transactions between AT&T, Lucent, and NCR were laid out in a separation and distribution agreement. Lucent Technologies was divested in a two-step process. Initially, 17 percent of the company was sold to investors in a $3 billion IPO on April 4, 1996. Six months later, on September 30, the remaining 83 percent of Lucent was given to AT&T shareholders as a tax-free dividend in an IRC Section 355 spin-off. On December 31, 1996, shares of NCR Corporation were distributed to AT&T shareholders as a tax-free spin-off.

Lucent Technologies

Lucent Technologies is the world's largest designer, developer, and manufacturer of communications systems, software, and products. It is a global leader in the sale of public communications systems, business communications systems, microelectronic components for communication systems, and computers. The company has 46 manufacturing and repair sites in 19 countries and field service offices in 47 countries. It gains more than 20 percent of its revenues from outside the United States.

As of December 31, 1995, Lucent had 131,000 employees, 82 percent of whom were in the United States. Of the U.S. employees, 47 percent were represented by unions, primarily the Communications Workers of America and the International Brotherhood of Electrical Workers. Per the restructuring plan discussed below, 22,000 positions (11,000 management and 11,000 occupational) were to be eliminated within the next two years.

Revenues for the year ending December 31, 1995, were $21.4 billion, with the following segment breakdown: network systems (54 percent), business communications systems (24 percent), microelectronic products (9 percent), consumer products (8 percent), and sales to the U.S. government (5 percent). Summary financial data for the five years ended 1995 are provided in table 9. This reflects operating results as well as pretax restructuring charges in 1991 and 1995 and a 1993 accounting change. The table also provides the operating results alone without the restructuring and accounting charges. The data indicate gross margins in the 40 percent range. Revenues in recent years have been growing in the 8 to 10 percent range.

NCR

NCR was merged into AT&T on September 19, 1991. NCR designs, markets, and services information technology products, services, systems, and solutions on a global basis. NCR offers information technology systems, such as point-of-sale workstations; barcode scanning equipment; transactions processing solutions; data storage, manipulation, and usage; computer platforms, systems, and workstations; network servers; software systems; imaging and payment systems and self-service devices such as ATMs; and business forms, ink ribbons, and other products and supplies. NCR operates through five business units: the computer systems group, the financial systems group, the retail systems group, worldwide services, and Systemedia. As of December 31, 1995, worldwide services and the computer systems group provided 36 percent and 35 percent of revenues, respectively.

As of December 31, 1995, NCR reported revenues of $8.2 billion and a net loss of $2.28 billion, including a restructuring charge of $1.65 billion. These figures illustrate NCR's troubled past: The unit had

Table 9
Lucent Technologies
Statement of Operations Data ($ millions)

| | \multicolumn{5}{c}{Year Ended December 31,} | | | | |
	1995	1994	1993	1992	1991
Revenues	$ 21,413	$ 19,765	$ 17,734	$ 17,312	$ 16,312
Costs[a]	12,945	11,337	10,088	10,383	9,385
Gross margin	8,468	8,428	7,646	6,929	6,927
Operating expenses					
Selling, general, and administrative expenses[a,b]	7,083	5,360	5,016	4,814	6,241
Research and development expenses[a]	2,385	2,097	1,961	1,711	1,996
Operating income (loss)	(1,000)	971	669	404	(1,310)
Income (loss) before income taxes and cumulative effects of accounting changes	(1,116)	854	666	302	(1,529)
Cumulative effects of accounting changes			(4,208)		
Net income (loss)[a]	(853)	523	(3,750)	194	(975)

[a]1995 includes pretax restructuring and other charges of $2,801 ($1,847 after taxes) recorded as $892 of costs, $1,645 of selling, general and administrative expenses, and $264 of research and development expenses.

[b]1991 includes pretax restructuring and other charges of $1,006 ($612 after taxes).

shown a profit in only one year and had accumulated losses in excess of $3.5 billion. At year-end 1995, NCR had 41,100 employees worldwide.

Management Teams

As in other successful divestitures, getting an experienced management team in place was essential. Within a month of the split-up announcement, AT&T introduced the new management teams for the three new companies.

At the new AT&T, Alex Mandl, who had headed AT&T's main Communications Services division, was named president and chief operating officer (COO). Mandl, who joined AT&T in 1991 from Sea-Land Service Inc., was AT&T's CFO before taking over Communications Services and was instrumental in AT&T's push into the wireless world, including the acquisition of McCaw Cellular. (He eventually left AT&T within the next year.) Three other key positions were filled within a month. Gail McGovern, a longtime AT&T employee, was named EVP and head of the $20 billion Business Services division. John Petrillo, another longtime AT&T employee, was named EVP in charge of business strategy. Pier Carlo Falotti, new to AT&T, was appointed EVP in charge of international operations. Other significant appointments included Joseph Nacchio, EVP–Consumer and Small Business division; Ron Ponder, EVP and chief information officer; Steve Hooper, president and CEO of AT&T Wireless; David Hunt, president of AT&T Universal Card Services; and Victor Millar, president of AT&T Solutions.

At Lucent Technologies, Henry Schacht, an AT&T board member for 11 years and the former CEO of Cummins Engine, was named chairman and CEO. Richard McGinn, formerly EVP and CEO of the Network Systems unit, was named president and COO. Allen viewed these positions as critical, and Schacht's experience in running a public company, his previous success in the legendary turnaround at Cummins, and his outstanding reputation on Wall Street were key to his appointment.

A challenging position—CEO of the new NCR—went to Lars Nyberg. Nyberg was previously head of Phillips Electronics Communications Systems Division and was viewed by most as an unknown quantity. The Global Information Systems Division, or GIS, as NCR was known at AT&T, had been somewhat of a disaster since its purchase in 1991 for $7.4 billion. Despite AT&T's capital investment and a large push to compete with IBM, HP, and others, GIS suffered from operational and marketing problems, lost millions of dollars, and was still primarily known as a purveyor of checkout systems at retail outlets.

The Lucent Divestiture

Lucent's IPO and Capitalization

Lucent's $3.0 billion IPO was the largest in U.S. financial history. Due to its size, investment bankers competed intensely for the business. AT&T chose Morgan Stanley and Goldman, Sachs as joint global coordinators, with Merrill Lynch as senior co-manager. The April 4, 1996, IPO was priced at $27, well above the $22 to $25 range established when the IPO was filed, due to tremendous investor interest. The 112-million share deal was oversubscribed by nearly five times and finished trading at $30.50 on day 1. Lucent's stock price continued to climb over the following month and closed on April 30 at $36.

Lucent retained the IPO proceeds. However, as part of the capitalization plan, AT&T had issued $4 billion in commercial paper, which was then assumed by Lucent. In addition, AT&T retained approximately $2.0 billion in receivables as part of the separation agreement. Finally, AT&T set up a working capital facility with Chemical Bank, which gave Lucent the ability to borrow up to $3 billion, the outstanding portion of which was repaid with proceeds from the IPO.

The IPO was part of the capitalization plan devised for Lucent. As indicated by Lawrence Prendergast, then AT&T vice president and treasurer, "We basically worked backwards. We wanted to achieve a strong A-bond rating for Lucent. In addition, we had to consider a number of other factors, including the company's prospective financing requirements, working capital and capital expenditure requirements, R&D expenditures, and customer financing needs." The December 31, 1995, pro forma capitalization for Lucent is illustrated in table 10.

AT&T sought to have its trivestiture treated as a tax-free distribution under Section 355 of the code for both the distribution of the 83 percent of Lucent shares and the 100 percent distribution of NCR shares. As such, none of the companies or shareholders would recognize a taxable gain or loss in the transaction. One requirement of Section 355 is that five years of financial performance figures be compiled. "Gathering and putting together the accounting data to comply with Section 355 was very cumbersome," noted Prendergast.

Table 10
Lucent Technologies Capitalization (Pro forma at December 31, 1995)

Short-term debt	
Debt maturing within one year	$49
Debt from commercial paper assumption	+3,842
Total short-term debt	$3,891
Long-term debt (including capital leases)	$123
Stockholders' equity	+2,334
Total capitalization	$2,457

The Lucent divestiture required a major restructuring of business processes as well as a shift in management and personnel. In the fourth quarter of 1995, a pretax charge of $2.8 billion was recorded for restructuring and asset impairment costs. The restructuring involved major process improvements in the design, manufacture, and distribution of consumer products. Included were the closing of retail phone centers, consolidation of business unit operations, and the sales of the Microelectronics interconnect and Paradyne businesses. Separation costs for almost 22,000 managerial and operational employees as well as costs associated with lease terminations and asset write-downs were also included. These total charges reduced net income by $1.85 billion and left the company with a net loss of $853 million for 1995. However, the restructuring was expected to cut costs by almost $1.5 billion in two years.

Corporate Governance

When planning the Lucent divestiture, AT&T put in place a designated board of directors. "The role of this board was to prepare the company to go public," said Prendergast. The slate of directors as of the IPO date is listed in table 11.

All of the Lucent board members listed in table 11 were either AT&T board members or employees. The five directors who were also AT&T board members resigned from the AT&T board on the IPO closing date, April 4, 1996. The seven directors who were AT&T employees (indicated with an asterisk in table 11) resigned from the Lucent board on the date of the spin-off, September 30, 1996.

Table 11
AT&T's Slate of Directors for Lucent Technologies

Name	Positions and Offices Held
Henry B. Schacht	Chairman and CEO, Lucent Technologies; AT&T board member since 1981
Richard A. McGinn	President and COO, Lucent Technologies; former EVP and CEO of AT&T Network Systems Group
Carla A. Hills	AT&T director since 1993; CEO of Hills & Co.; former U.S. trade representative
Drew Lewis	AT&T director since 1989; chairman and CEO of Union Pacific Corporation since 1987; former U.S. secretary of transportation
Donald S. Perkins	AT&T director since 1979; former chairman and CEO of Jewel Companies
Franklin A. Thomas	AT&T director since 1988; president of the Ford Foundation since 1979
*Ephraim M. Brecher	Vice president–Taxes and Tax Law, AT&T; joined board as of IPO
*Jim G. Kilpatric	Senior vice president–Law, AT&T; joined board as of IPO
*Marc E. Manley	Vice president–Law, and solicitor general, AT&T; joined board as of IPO
*S. Lawrence Prendergast	Vice president and treasurer, AT&T; joined board as of IPO
*Maureen B. Tart	Vice president and controller, AT&T; joined board February 6, 1996
*Florence L. Walsh	Assistant treasurer, AT&T; joined board as of IPO
*Paul J. Wondrasch	Senior vice president, AT&T International; joined board as of IPO

*Only on Lucent board until spin-off from AT&T on September 30, 1996.

Division of Assets

Depending on the assets in question, their division in divestitures can be quite simple or quite difficult and complex. In the AT&T trivestiture, physical assets such as plants and buildings went to the division that occupied them. In some cases, especially in and around headquarters in Basking Ridge, New Jersey, AT&T and Lucent actually shared buildings, with ownership going to the primary tenant and a short-term lease to the secondary tenant.

Bell Labs had more complex asset-division issues. Since its founding in 1925, an average of one patent per day has been issued to Bell Labs. Its technological achievements have included sound motion pictures (1928); the transistor (1947); the laser (1958); the communications satellite (1962); and the cellular telephone (1978). Seven scientists from Bell Labs have won the Nobel Prize in physics. AT&T annually allocated an R&D budget of nearly 7 percent of revenues to this valuable resource. Per the separation agreement, Lucent retained about 75 percent of Bell Labs and its 26,000 employees. The units associated with Bell Labs were integrated into Lucent's operating units in design, development, and manufacturing engineering. The remainder of Bell Labs, which had focused on communications services, went to AT&T. From this remnant of Bell Labs, the new AT&T created AT&T Labs to spearhead its R&D activities.

Patents proved to be another difficult asset-division issue. "We had over 10,000 patents at the time of the divestiture, and there were many cross-licensing agreements between AT&T, Lucent, and NCR," said Prendergast. Lucent retained approximately 8,000 patents.

Human Resources

Reallocating employees between AT&T and Lucent was not overly difficult. Management personnel involved in providing communications services went to AT&T, and those with equipment responsibilities went to Lucent. Separating management personnel in support areas such as treasury, accounting, law, and human resources was more difficult.

Employee benefits, pension funds, and compensation can become important issues in company split-ups. In the AT&T–Lucent split-up, Lucent employees retained virtually the same benefit and pension package they had with AT&T. Lucent also adopted a long-term incentive plan for executives prior to the IPO. Officers and directors did have options and stock awards totaling 4 million shares of AT&T stock, which were converted (unless exercised) to the appropriate number of Lucent options and stock awards at the spin-off.

Transition Period Agreements

The separation and distribution agreement included a number of arrangements and agreements between AT&T and Lucent for the transition period. Depending on the arrangement or agreement, the transition period was one to three years. Areas covered such matters as tax allocation, tax sharing, and real estate agreements, as well as procedures to address issues like dispute resolution and contingent liabilities and gains. For example, the separation and distribution agreement indemnified Lucent, AT&T, and NCR on contingent liabilities from their related business activities, subject to certain sharing provisions. These provisions stipulated sharing of contingent liabilities above $100 million as follows:

1. AT&T: AT&T pays 75 percent, Lucent pays 22 percent, and NCR pays 3 percent.

2. Lucent: AT&T pays 47 percent, Lucent pays 50 percent, and NCR pays 3 percent.

3. NCR: AT&T pays 37 percent, Lucent pays 13 percent, and NCR pays 50 percent.

The agreement also provided for sharing and, in some cases, jointly owning, certain technologies, brand licenses, and patent licenses for a certain period. For example, the patent license agreement provided for royalty-free cross licenses for AT&T and Lucent to "use, sell, lease, and import any and all products and services of the business in which the licensed company (including specified related companies) is now or hereafter engaged." The cross licenses cover all of each company's patents on patent applications filed before December 31, 1996. The technology license agreement was similar to the patent license agreement.

The purchase agreements were very significant. Under these agreements, AT&T agreed to purchase $3 billion in products and services from Lucent through December 31, 1998. This agreement provided an assurance that AT&T would purchase Lucent's communications equipment during a short transition period.

Post-Divestiture Performance

Industry competitors and stock analysts were fairly bullish on the post-divestiture prospects for Lucent and AT&T. Most observers also believed that an independent, restructured Lucent Technologies would thrive in the fast-growing communications equipment market. In addition, many believed that a sleeker, more focused AT&T would invade the local service market to the detriment of the Baby Bells. Specifically, they highlighted AT&T's one-stop service that packaged long-distance with wireless services. Salomon Brothers analyst Jack Grubman noted, "The new AT&T will be one of the world-class providers of integrated, bundled, end-to-end service solutions." Virtually all stock analysts assessed the value of AT&T, Lucent, and NCR in excess of the parent's $63.75 post-announcement stock price.

Lucent's performance after the IPO was extraordinary. As shown in figure 9, the stock price has significantly increased, as its split-adjusted price increased from $13.50 per share as of the IPO to $66 over the first 24 months. In the process, Lucent's 1997 sales and net income have grown to $26.36 billion and $1.5 billion, respectively, with a return on

Figure 9
Lucent Stock Performance

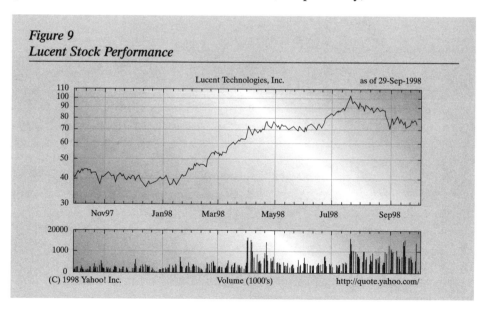

equity of 44.5 percent, market-to-book ratio of more than 20, and a total market capitalization in excess of $80 billion. Through 1997, Lucent continually outperformed market expectations. Table 12 shows projected data from Value Line Investment Surveys dated July 12, 1996, and April 10, 1998.

Summing up the company's success in reporting a tripling of the previous year's quarterly results, Schacht noted, "These great results reflect accelerating growth in our core markets and show that we are making the right moves to solidify our position as a high-growth, high-performance company. We've again generated strong revenues and improved our cost structure to significantly improve our bottom line." In particular, in sales of switching and wireless systems and software and fiber optic cable to network operators, revenue growth was more than 25 percent over the previous year. Sales of such equipment were deemed in jeopardy before the spin-off because the former Lucent was a subsidiary of AT&T. Lucent also reported revenue growth rates of 14 percent for microelectronic products, 16 percent for business communications systems, and 30 percent for consumer products. Gross margins were up to

Table 12
Lucent Technologies Statements of Income ($ millions)

		July 12, 1996		April 10, 1998	
	1996 Actual	1997 Projected	2000 Projected	1997 Actual	2002 Projected
Sales	$23,450	$25,450	$31,500	$26,360	$48,880
Operating Margin	9.0%	16.5%	18.0%	15.4%	17.5%
Net Income	$224	$1,320	$1,980	$1,507	$3,765
Return on Equity	8.3%	20.5%	17.5%	44.5%	22.0%
Earnings Per Share	$.19	$2.05	$3.05	$1.55	$2.80

Source: Value Line

41 percent, attributed to productivity improvements. Capital expenditures grew 50 percent, and R&D expenses made up 12 percent of sales.

According to Peter Sperling, the treasury director for capital markets at Lucent, the company's exceptional performance can be traced to several factors. First, investors recognized that Lucent would be a more nimble competitor. Second, investors could identify the promise of the equipment business without having to deal with the turmoil in communications services. Third, the management team headed by Schacht and McGinn provided strong leadership from the beginning, with a very clear strategy and vision. Finally, Lucent exceeded expectations, especially on a cash flow basis.

Three other notable changes occurred after the divestiture. First, notes Sperling, "From day one, the company was focused on cash flow and value creation." Second, executives were required to take more risk in their compensation packages, with options replacing salary. (For example, Schacht's salary was a relatively modest $900,000 per year.) Third, Lucent was very active in acquisition and joint venture activity, as divested firms tend to be. In 1997, Lucent announced several significant joint ventures, including one with U.S. Venture Partners to form Veridicom, a company that will make personal identification products using Bell Labs-patented fingerprint authentication technology; one with USA Digital Radio to develop digital broadcasting technologies for FM and AM transmission and reception; and a joint venture to combine communications products businesses with Philips Electronics N.V. In addition, the company made a significant acquisition in Octel Communications, a leader in voice, fax, and electronic messaging technologies, for $1.8 billion in cash.

AT&T and NCR's post-split-up performances have not been nearly as impressive (see figures 10 and 11). AT&T stumbled as John Walter, Allen's handpicked successor, resigned one year after joining the firm. Michael Armstrong was then brought in, to the delight of Wall Street. With both top-line growth and margins in the rough-and-tumble market for communications services, AT&T's stock began to perform better in 1997 as its prospects clearly picked up with the $12.5 billion acquisition

Figure 10
AT&T Stock Performance

Figure 11
NCR Stock Performance

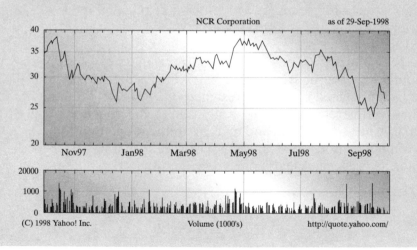

of Teleport Communications. Teleport is a leader in the local business market, with a presence in 66 large metropolitan areas.

NCR has experienced a modest decline in revenues and stock price since its December 1996 spin-off. While NCR reduced costs 22 percent in its first two years as an independent company, its two largest divisions—customer services and computer products—have both experienced revenue declines of nearly 10 percent. Revenues have also been affected by the loss of $45 million in sales to AT&T.

DuPont's Carve-Out
of Photomasks

Introduction

Dupont Photomasks was a wholly owned subsidiary of E.I. du Pont de Nemours and Company and one of two dominant mask producers in the U.S. market. These two firms each had about 40 percent of the U.S. market prior to DuPont's IPO. (The masks are glass plates used to etch microscopic circuitry onto semiconductor wafers. Sketches of the circuitry are first put onto the glass masks and then transferred to silicon chips.) The subsidiary was considered to be a poor performer within the DuPont organization, and a plan was developed to take it public in summer 1997. Through an initial public offering, DuPont sold 30 percent of the outstanding Photomasks shares and retained the other 70 percent. Since the IPO, DuPont Photomasks has been operating as an independent company with its own board of directors. The original plan was for DuPont to divest itself of the remaining 70 percent stake over time. However, Photomasks has performed well, and DuPont currently seems content to maintain its 70 percent stake.

In the discussion that follows, the parent company is referred to as DuPont and the carved-out subsidiary is referred to as Photomasks. However, due to a trade name and trademark agreement, the subsidiary uses the full name DuPont Photomasks, Inc. Also, some post-IPO contracts and agreements are between Photomasks and DuPont Chemical and Energy Operations, Inc., a wholly owned subsidiary of DuPont. To simplify the discussion, we make no distinction between DuPont and this subsidiary.

Background

Photomasks and Photronics are the dominant photomask manufacturers, accounting for about 80 percent of the U.S. market. Photomasks believes it is the primary supplier for Advanced MicroDevices, Delco/General Motors Digital, Hyundai, LG Semicon, Lucent Technologies, Micron Technology, Motorola, National Semiconductor, Philips, Samsung, Seagate, and SGS-Thomson. In 1995, over 40 percent of Photomasks' sales were to only four companies, and about two-thirds of its sales were to its ten largest customers. Thus, the loss of a few key customers could seriously affect the financial health of the company. Of course, upside potential is also enormous if the company wins a small number of supply contracts with large semiconductor manufacturers.

Before the carve-out, there had been excess capacity in the photomask industry, but after a long shakeout, that excess has been trimmed. The industry now seems to be in a good position for growth and expansion. Photomasks' top management had been located in Wilmington, Delaware, but with the IPO has moved to Austin, Texas. In Photomasks' last year as a wholly owned DuPont subsidiary, sales totaled $150 million with about 1,000 employees. Although profitable, the subsidiary was deemed a poor performer that really did not fit well with DuPont's other operations.

The categorization of "poor fit" encompassed several points. Management at both DuPont and Photomasks frequently mentioned the very fast cycle times the photomask industry requires and noted that it is very capital intensive. DuPont is structured to allocate capital to its business units on the basis of their projections, typically submitted on an annual basis. Events in the photomask business are so volatile and fast changing that Photomasks managers felt the need to make significant capital expenditures without the lead time the parent organization required. DuPont managers referred to Photomasks' "insatiable capital needs" as a problem. Photomasks was considered a nonstrategic unit within DuPont and therefore not able to attract adequate quantities of new investment capital.

Employees in the Photomasks unit felt that a more entrepreneurial management style would be required to successfully guide the unit through the next decade. Organizations within the semiconductor industry and the various firms serving it comprise a culture that is very entrepreneurial and youth oriented. The average age of Photomasks employees is much younger than the average for those at DuPont. These younger workers seem to demand stock-based incentives as part of their pay package. DuPont could not provide incentives to these workers with stock representing their performance in the photomask business without the planned IPO.

The photomask industry is very customer oriented, and customer needs change rapidly. New capital investments sometimes need to be made within weeks of changing customer needs. This was difficult to do within the capital allocation scheme of the much larger parent organization. DuPont does provide other services to chip manufacturers, but our discussions with DuPont managers indicate that the photomask activities were never synergistic with other DuPont business units. In summary, Photomasks was not performing well as a wholly owned subsidiary, could not raise adequate amounts of investment capital within the parent company, and needed a more entrepreneurial management style in order to respond quickly to changing customer needs. Allowing Photomasks to operate as a separate company seemed a reasonable solution.

The Plan

In June 1996, an IPO of 4 million shares of Photomasks was carried out at an offering price of $17 per share. After this IPO, Photomasks was projected to have 14.5 million shares outstanding. Of that total, DuPont would own 10.5 million, and the remaining 4 million would be held by the public. Thus, DuPont would hold 72 percent of the outstanding shares, which gave the parent company a controlling interest in the carved-out subsidiary. The underwriters were Morgan Stanley & Co., Cowen & Co., and Needham & Company, Inc.

The underwriting contract contained a "green shoe provision," whereby the underwriters held an option to buy an additional 600,000 shares at the offering price of $17 a share. The option, if exercised, would increase the number of shares under public ownership by 15 percent. The purpose of the green shoe provision was to allow underwriters to secure commitments for more than the original allotment of 4 million shares. Experience shows that more investors express a willingness to buy new issues than actually buy them. By getting more commitments than shares offered for sale, the underwriters increase the likelihood that the issue will be fully subscribed. However, the underwriters are exposed to the risk that they will have committed themselves to sell more shares than are being issued. The green shoe provision allows them to exercise their option and fill all orders. In the Photomasks IPO, the green shoe option was exercised and an additional 600,000 shares were sold to the public, bringing the total in public hands to 4.6 million and lowering DuPont's percentage ownership to about 70 percent.

IPOs are classified as primary or secondary, depending on whether the shares offered for sale are owned by an independent investor or are sold directly by the company. For example, DuPont initially owned 10.5 million shares of Photomasks. If DuPont were to sell some of these shares, the offering would be classified as a secondary offering. However, new shares in Photomasks were created and sold by Photomasks, thus making this a primary offering.

Costs

While the offering price to the public was $17 a share, the underwriters bought their shares from Photomasks at a $1.19 discount, or $15.81 a share. This discount is typically deemed to be a cost to the issuer, because the issuer is selling something worth $17 but only realizing $15.81. Although Photomasks was promised $15.81 a share, the company promised the underwriters $660,000 in direct expenses. Including shares sold due to the green shoe option, the total price to the public was $78.2 million ($17 a share times 4.6 million shares). Underwriting discounts totaled $5,474,000 ($1.19 a share times 4.6 million shares) and, when additional expenses of $660,000 are included, the underwriting take totaled $6,134,000. Photomasks' net proceeds totaled $72,066,000.

Use of Funds

The investment community was well aware of DuPont's intention to buy back the large block of shares held by Seagrams. However, DuPont management made it very clear and public that the sale of Photomasks' stock to the public was not part of its share buyback plan. Of the amount raised through the offering, $9.1 million was to be retained by Photomasks, with the remaining funds used to repay indebtedness to DuPont Chemical and Energy Operations, Inc., a wholly owned subsidiary of DuPont. It is interesting to note that although this IPO is classified as a primary offering, the parent company is receiving a large percentage of the proceeds by virtue of the debt refunding transaction. The funds retained by Photomasks will be available for general corporate purposes, including capital expenditures and working capital.

The New Management Team

The new CEO of Photomasks, Mike Hardinger, was appointed in December 1995, about six months before the IPO. Several DuPont managers believe that the new CEO should have been appointed earlier in the process. Many key decisions about the structure of the carved-out entity had been made long before his appointment.

The original Photomasks board of directors consisted of 14 members. Six of those were full-time employees of Photomasks. Five were full-time employees of DuPont, and two of them had significant experience in the electronic materials business. The director of human development for DuPont was one of these five board members, probably owing to the human resources issues involved in managing and severing the link between the 1,000 Photomasks employees and the parent company in areas such as pension and health benefits. Three outside directors had no prior connection to either DuPont or Photomasks. Two had long careers in computer engineering design or manufacturing activities, and one was active in the venture capital area.

Even though a great deal of DuPont working experience was present on this board, DuPont did not hold a majority. Hardinger described the board as both competent and independent of DuPont. Clearly, DuPont could seize control of the board at any moment simply by virtue of its 70 percent ownership of Photomasks' stock. However, managers at both DuPont and Photomasks felt that this board was free of the subtle coercion that could influence a board made up of only DuPont employees. They believed DuPont could exercise total control over Photomasks only by replacing Photomasks executives.

5

What Was Different After the Carve-Out

An interview with Photomasks' Hardinger revealed substantial differences in operations as a result of the ECO. Hardinger felt that decision making was much faster and less cumbersome because it was no longer necessary to gain approval within the larger DuPont organization. One specific area of improvement, in Hardinger's opinion, was the level of capital expenditures. As a wholly owned subsidiary of DuPont, Photomasks was investing about $20 million a year in capital equipment. Hardinger estimated that the company needed at least $40 million a year just to maintain its position. For 1997, Photomasks' capital expenditures totaled $52 million, and capital expenditures for 1998 are projected to be approximately $70 million. Hardinger was quick to point out that internally generated cash flow ought to be able to support this level of capital expenditures.

While decision making is less cumbersome under the carve-out arrangement, Hardinger finds himself spending a great deal of time communicating his plans and projections to the investment community. This is a trade-off that both pleases him and is necessary. Before the carve-out, managers of the parent company communicated with the individual business units and then summarized the relevant data for distribution to the investment community. Now, Hardinger must distribute his information directly to the investing public.

Hardinger finds the existence of publicly traded Photomasks stock of great benefit for several reasons. One is the availability of a daily scorekeeper to let Photomasks' managers evaluate their own performance. Another reason is the presence of an important incentive-producing device in the form of stock grants and stock options. In addition to a fairly standard package of stock options for top management, stock options were made available for all employees and the nonemployee members of Photomasks' board of directors. Whether DuPont employees serving on the Photomasks board will receive options is not clear.

Compensation Plans

The stated purpose of the nonemployee directors' stock option plan is to allow for recruiting and retaining highly competent outside directors. Each outside director receives options to purchase 10,000 shares either upon joining the board or on the date of the IPO, whichever is later.

These directors receive annual options on an additional 3,000 shares of Photomasks. Hardinger repeatedly referred to the substantial contributions by outside board members. This stock option plan clearly demonstrates that Photomasks values their contributions.

Photomasks' board of directors also instituted a founders' stock option plan. Under this plan, nearly all employees of the company were awarded options to acquire 252 shares of common stock at an exercise price equal to the offering price of the IPO. These options would vest at the rate of 25 percent a year, so that after four years, the employees would hold vested interests in options for 252 shares of common stock.

The Photomasks prospectus indicated that significant quantities of restricted stock and options on common stock would be used to provide incentives for top management to create value. The CEO was to receive restricted stock worth $242,000 and stock options with an exercise price equal to the initial offer price of $17 per share. The stock options granted to the CEO had an aggregate exercise price of $2,475,000 and would represent options on over 145,000 common shares of Photomasks. Other officers received options ranging from just over 11,000 shares to about 88,000 shares.

Before the ECO, Photomasks' employees were covered under DuPont's defined benefit retirement plan. Photomasks' management believed this plan would not attract the young, talented people their business needed. Photomasks' competitors for labor tend to offer defined contribution plans, making Photomasks' benefits package less attractive. Worker turnover within the semiconductor business tends to be relatively high. If workers come to Photomasks from firms with defined contribution plans and then leave the company, their few years at Photomasks covered by a defined benefits plan will not contribute substantially to their overall retirement package. Therefore, as part of the carve-out arrangements, management replaced the defined benefit plan with a defined contribution plan.

Contractual Arrangements in Place Between DuPont and Photomasks After the IPO

Before the IPO, DuPont and Photomasks stated their intent to enter into several service agreements after the offering was completed. These agreements were in such areas as cash management, accounting, computer and information systems, and employee benefits administration. Other key agreements are described in the following paragraphs.

The two companies established a research, development, and consulting agreement. DuPont's obligation was to supply Photomasks with relevant analytical support and specified consulting assistance as needed. Photomasks agreed to pay $100,000 annually for these services. If the cost of these services exceeds $100,000, Photomasks must either pay the additional costs or refuse the services. Clearly, the ECO was consummated with the intent of having Photomasks rely on DuPont's vast array of technical and administrative expertise.

Photomasks and DuPont also entered into a credit arrangement whereby DuPont promised to provide revolving credit/working capital loan arrangements. The amount was for up to $30 million, and the agreement was for 24 months, beginning with the IPO. The loan rate to be charged was pegged at the London Interbank Offered Rate (LIBOR) plus 50 basis points, to be adjusted every six months. Any loan under this agreement would be secured by Photomasks' assets.

Other agreements included an environmental indemnification agreement and a corporate trade name and trademark agreement. The former was to deal with any lawsuits involving environmental contamination. DuPont agreed to indemnify Photomasks for any environmental contamination present on Photomasks' manufacturing sites prior to the IPO. Also, in cases in which DuPont and Photomasks could not agree on when the contamination occurred, DuPont promised to indemnify Photomasks for all suits brought within one year after the IPO. Many ECOs involve subsidiaries with environmental contamination issues, and this indemnification agreement appears to be unique.

One key aspect of the trade name and trademark agreement allows Photomasks to use the corporate name "DuPont Photomasks, Inc." Hardinger is of the opinion that this agreement helped his salespeople obtain necessary appointments, especially in the Far East. The DuPont name is highly visible worldwide and is of considerable value to Photomasks.

Performance Subsequent to the IPO

Measurable performance improved substantially after the IPO of stock in Photomasks. Sales are up considerably and earnings are somewhat higher. Annual capital expenditures have more than doubled since the carve-out and may triple if 1998 projections are met. Photomasks' stock-price performance has been highly volatile. From $17 a share in June 1996, share price rose to an all-time high of $72 by September 1997. That increase represents an annual return of about 217 percent. However, in October 1997 the share price fell back into the $30 to $40 range and subsequently fell into the high $20s. The stock finished 1997 at $34.875.

DuPont estimated Photomasks' value to be about $300 million prior to the IPO. DuPont believed it could receive only $200 million in an outright sale of the unit. Thus, DuPont hoped to realize more of Photomasks' intrinsic value through the public offering. At the offering price of $17, Photomasks was valued at about $256.7 million. Using the 1997 closing figure of $34.875, the aggregate value of the firm is about $526 million. Based on its own estimates, DuPont has captured significant value enhancement through this carve-out. Of course, the photomask business is highly volatile. The very small number of customers and major contracts held by Photomasks imply that any large change in value (either up or down) could have taken place independent of the IPO.

Summary

What

In June 1996, DuPont's wholly owned subsidiary, DuPont Photomasks, Inc., sold 4.6 million shares of its common stock in a primary IPO. The offering price was $17 a share.

Why

DuPont management was unhappy with the performance of this subsidiary. Management believed that (1) there were no synergies with other DuPont operations, (2) the culture of the photomasks industry was a bad fit with the DuPont culture, and (3) Photomasks would have greater value externally. DuPont management also believed that Photomasks required capital expenditures far in excess of what DuPont wanted to allocate to a non-core business unit.

Cost

Underwriting discounts and commissions	$5,474,000
Fixed payment to the underwriters	660,000
Estimated expense within DuPont	6,000,000
Total	$12,134,000

Approximate Use of Proceeds

To Photomasks for general corporate purposes	$9,100,000
To reduce debt owed DuPont	$63,000,000

Key Outcomes

Decision making was streamlined.

Stock-based incentives tied to Photomasks' performance became available.

Photomasks' board of directors could act independently of DuPont.

Results

DuPont's and Photomasks' managements judge the transaction to be a success.

Sales are up substantially.

Capital expenditures will probably quadruple in 1998 over 1995.

Stock quadrupled in value and then fell back to about 100 percent above the offering price after 18 months.

Marriott Splits into Host Marriott and Marriott International

Introduction

The early 1990s found the hotel industry in a slump, with hotel market values at historically low levels. The Marriott Corporation was over-leveraged and in need of new capital infusions to maintain a growth strategy of building and then selling new hotels. At this time, management decided on a different strategy, in which growth would result from a rapid expansion of Marriott's management business. The strategy of building and selling new hotels would be discontinued. Management decided to ameliorate the constraints imposed by their overleveraged position through a spin-off of their hotel management business into a separate corporate entity to be named Marriott International. The original corporation would be renamed Host Marriott.

The planned spin-off called for most of the debt to remain with Host Marriott, allowing Marriott International to pursue its newly adopted growth strategy by rapidly increasing the number of hotels under management. Marriott International CFO Mike Stein[1] described the new strategy as capturing ever-increasing management fees with very little asset intensity. Concurrently, Host Marriott could grow its asset-intensive hotel ownership business. The spin-off created two separate entities, each capable of pursuing a strategy that would have conflicted with the other had there been no spin-off. Bondholders believed the plan increased their exposure to the risk of default, and they threatened legal action.

---

[1] At the time of the interview, Mr. Stein was CFO of Marriott International. He is now Executive Vice President and Chief Financial Officer of Nordstrom, Inc.

Background

In 1992, Marriott was generally considered to be a hotel company. Its two major activities were managing and owning hotels, with a large majority of the hotels under management not owned by Marriott. Hotels were constructed under Marriott ownership and then sold to other parties, with Marriott continuing to manage them under contract. Marriott sold primarily to syndicated partnerships, insurance companies, and international investors (especially Japanese). Marriott used the cash from hotel sales to finance construction of new hotels. However, in the early 1990s, growth in demand for hotel rooms slowed dramatically. Marriott's inventory of hotels developed for sale grew to an all-time high because it could not sell these properties at prices management deemed appropriate.

Average hotel sale prices peaked in 1988 at $80,000 per room, according to Hospitality Valuation Services. That average fell to about $35,000 by 1993. Historically low prices made it difficult for new construction to be profitable. Many owners of hotel property were reluctant to sell at these prices in hopes of a price rebound. This decline in the market value of Marriott's hotel inventory, coupled with less cash from hotel sales, led to lower debt ratings and a higher debt ratio for Marriott.

Management was committed to a policy of strong growth even while recession gripped the industry. However, Marriott's inability to sell new hotels put pressure on corporate cash flows. This problem was further exacerbated by a general economic downturn, accompanied by lower hotel revenues. Marriott's debt policy was to finance most of its capital requirements through notes and debentures rather than mortgage debt secured by new construction. In 1992, the total amount of mortgage debt Marriott used was less than $500 million, compared with $1.872 billion worth of senior notes and debentures outstanding. This use of general corporate obligations rather than mortgage debt provided much more flexibility to buy and sell hotels but made it very difficult for Marriott to continue its construction programs in the face of a deteriorating hotel market.

The resulting higher debt ratio and declining bond ratings made additional debt financing very costly. An infusion of equity capital was not an attractive alternative for at least two reasons. The Marriott family held about 25 percent of the stock; they did not want to issue additional shares, thereby diluting their control. As one indication of this reluctance to tap equity markets, Marriott's number of shares outstanding actually declined by almost 30 percent between 1982 and 1991. In addition, issuing new equity would lower the debt ratio and raise the value of existing bonds, having the effect of transferring value from stockholders to bondholders. Ironically, high debt ratios can lead to a situation in which neither debt nor equity financing of new activities is a good alternative.

The weak hotel market in the early 1990s and Marriott's reluctance to sell from its inventory put pressure on corporate cash flows. Further, it made it difficult to pursue the strategic plan of building new hotels, selling them, and entering into an agreement to manage them. Table 13 reveals that by 1992, Marriott had drastically reduced investment in new property development in an attempt to match the decline in proceeds from hotel sales.

At that time, Marriott's inventory of hotels developed for sale was at an all-time high. Thus, Marriott faced serious obstacles to any strategic plan calling for growth of its hotel business, whether growth was to be through ownership or through the management business. These obstacles, coupled with a reluctance on the part of the Marriott family to dilute its ownership position in the corporation, made the proposed spin-off seem attractive. Even without control issues, raising new equity to lessen cash constraints brought on by too much debt is seldom a reasonable choice. The new equity is likely to transfer value to the holders of the firm's risky debt.

Table 13
Marriott's Diminishing Hotel Investments ($ millions)

	1986	1987	1988	1989	1990	1991	1992
Proceeds from hotel sales	846	475	980	900	600	33	346
New property investment	567	691	957	890	733	199	46

Reasons for Spin-Off

Marriott management came to believe that their high debt ratio was impeding their ability to grow. Their newly adopted strategy called for growth of their management business, but the unavailability of external funds at reasonable rates was a problem. A plan was developed to spin off the hotel management aspects of the business into a separate corporation named Marriott International and leave most of the debt with the remaining real estate business of the parent under the new name Host Marriott. In 1997, Marriott International CFO Stein said of this plan, "The purpose was to reallocate debt capacity." The spin-off left Marriott International with low debt levels, and, consequently, the ability to grow faster through the construction (financed by debt) and sale of new hotels. Issuing new debt would not be a problem for Marriott International. Host Marriott would be left with a very high level of debt, but this was deemed appropriate for a real estate company. Management believed Host Marriott would have enough financial strength to weather the industry recession and then sell from its hotel inventory at attractive prices, if necessary.

Aside from the desire to "reallocate debt capacity," management felt the market did not value Marriott properly when the management and real estate businesses were bundled together. They observed that analysts applied earnings multiples to Marriott that were appropriate for a hotel management company but not for a real estate company. Because of large depreciation charges, real estate companies tend to report low earnings and are valued on their cash flow. It was for this reason that Marriott built and then sold hotels. Retaining ownership of the hotels would be a drag on corporate earnings, because the large depreciation charges related to hotel ownership would significantly diminish hotel management earnings. One way of getting more accurate valuations would be to spin off the management business from the real estate business. Robert Parsons, CFO of Host Marriott, said of the spin-off, "It will allow us to grow our real estate business while being valued on a cash flow basis."

One other reason for the spin-off was a desire to sharpen corporate focus. The skills required to run a management company differ greatly from those required to run a real estate company. The real estate operation could be very lean. In fact, by 1997, the $6 billion Host Marriott had only 200 employees, while Marriott International had about 200,000 employees. Clearly, Host Marriott was a lean operation focused entirely on real estate. The management team at Marriott International felt they were better able to concentrate their efforts on the management side of the business.

The Original Spin-Off Proposal

The original plan was announced in October 1992 and called for the hotel management business, along with food service and other less significant activities, to be spun off into Marriott International. The parent company would be renamed Host Marriott and would retain ownership in virtually all of the property owned by the original Marriott Corporation. Table 14 shows the proposed division of the long-term debt between Marriott International and Host Marriott, along with the projected interest coverage ratios.

Clearly, the proposed division of debt concerned the Marriott bondholders, because most of the debt was assigned to Host Marriott. This assignment left the bondholders with claims to a firm with a substantially higher debt ratio, and the degree of interest coverage had been halved. This reallocation of debt need not hurt the bondholders, as noted by Marriott management. If the restructuring led to greatly improved operating performance at both remaining firms, then the bondholders could

Table 14
Original Spin-Off Proposal

	Marriott Corporation	Marriott International projected	Host Marriott projected
Long-term debt ($ millions)	2,890	20	2,870
Book debt/total capital	.88	.78	.95
Times interest earned	2.6	20.3	1.3

feel more secure in the knowledge that their claims would be satisfied from the enhanced cash flow. Marriott management focused its attention on its duties to Marriott shareholders, emphasizing once again that the spin-off would allow the company to fulfill its strategic plan to grow the hotel management business. Also, management felt the spin-off would allow the market to value the two components of their business more accurately.

Reaction to the Proposal and the Revised Plan

Marriott's stock price rose from $17.125 to $19.125 over the three-day period following the announcement of the proposed spin-off. This price increase of 11.7 percent occurred while the S&P Index was falling by about 2 percent. On the day of the announcement, Moody's lowered its rating of Marriott's senior debt, and price declines as large as 30 percent were noted on some debt issues. Robert Parrino, who wrote an article on the Marriott spin-off for the *Journal of Financial Economics,* estimated a decline in market value of $358 million for the senior debt plus preferred stock outstanding, an estimate that represented 14.35 percent of their combined values. Parrino estimated a value increase for the common shares of about $225 million. Thus, changes in market values at the time of the original announcement indicate that no additional value had been created. In fact, since the decline in debt and preferred stock values was larger than the increase in stock values by about $133 million, one might conclude that about $133 million of value was destroyed and that the source of increased value for shareholders was the reduction in the value of Marriott's senior debt and preferred stock.

On the day of the announcement, ten class action suits were filed against Marriott, and large bondholders were discussing ways to block the divestiture. The bondholders' major concern was a perception that Host Marriott carried too much debt and that default within a brief period was possible. In response to bondholders' actions, Marriott modified its proposal in several ways. More debt was allocated to Marriott International, a line of credit granted to Host Marriott by Marriott International was increased in value, and some debt was retired or defeased. These modifications led to better debt coverage at Host Marriott. Table 15 shows the new estimates for debt coverage.

Table 15
Revised Spin-Off Proposal

	Marriott Corporation	Marriott International projected	Host Marriott projected
Long-term debt ($ millions)	2,732	899	2,313
Book debt/total capital	.88	.85	.90
Times interest earned	2.8	6.5	1.8

The revised plan allocated more debt (and more assets) to Marriott International and reduced the interest coverage ratio at Marriott International. However, the bondholders were never concerned about their positions at that firm. Their concerns centered on the debt allocated to Host Marriott. The revised plan improved the claims of those bondholders by lowering the debt to total capital ratio and by substantially raising the amount of interest coverage.

The revised spin-off plan was approved by shareholders on July 23, 1993, and the distribution was completed on October 8 of the same year. Only two bondholder groups failed to reach agreement with Marriott by the distribution date. One group had a judgment entered against it after an inconclusive trial, and then settled with Marriott while its appeal was pending. The other (a Florida state pension fund) agreed to have its bonds repurchased at face value.

Timeline

■ **October 5, 1992**

Marriott announces the spin-off plan, which calls for shares representing ownership of the management businesses to be distributed to shareholders of the Marriott Corporation on a pro-rata basis. Moody's lowers its rating of both Marriott's senior debt and its subordinated debt. Ten class action suits are filed on behalf of Marriott's bondholders.

■ **October 29, 1992**

A group of investors holding Marriott senior debt files another lawsuit. The suit alleges that Marriott failed to disclose its restructuring plans when it issued senior notes in April 1992.

■ **November 12, 1992**

S&P announces its intention to downgrade Marriott debt when the spin-off occurs.

■ **November 17, 1992**

Merrill Lynch resigns as advisor to Marriott concerning the spin-off. Merrill Lynch had previously underwritten several Marriott debt issues.

■ **December 29, 1992**

Marriott announces that an effort is underway to resolve differences with its bondholders.

■ **January 13, 1993**

Marriott announces that projected earnings for 1992 will be higher than previously anticipated.

■ **January 25, 1993**

Marriott rejects bondholder proposals calling for Marriott International to cross guarantee Host Marriott's debt. Marriott offers to transfer real estate and its associated debt from Host to International to lessen the risk to bondholders.

■ **March 8, 1993**

Marriott announces its intention to amend the restructuring proposal.

■ **March 11, 1993**

Marriott announces its intention to modify its proposed spin-off to satisfy representatives of a large group of bondholders.

- **May 10, 1993**

  Marriott files its bond exchange offer with the SEC.

- **July 19, 1993**

  Marriott begins its debt exchange offer.

- **July 23, 1993**

  Marriott holds its annual shareholders' meeting. About 85 percent vote to approve the planned spin-off.

- **August 31, 1993**

  Marriott sets the record date for the spin-off as September 30 and the distribution date as October 8.

- **October 1, 1993**

  Marriott International begins trading on a when-issued basis.

- **October 8, 1993**

  Marriott issues shares of Marriott International as a stock dividend, thus separating the two companies and completing the spin-off.

Security Returns from Announcement to Distribution

For shareholders, two dates were of particular interest. As mentioned previously, the three-day period following the announcement of the proposed spin-off saw the stock rise more than 13 percent in value after adjusting for the performance of the overall market. The other interesting date is the day Merrill Lynch resigned as one of Marriott's advisors, because it was an underwriter for several of the bond issues in dispute. Marriott stock fell about 6 percent over the two-day period following the Merrill Lynch announcement, after adjusting for the performance of the overall market.

For the entire period from announcement through distribution, Marriott stock exhibited a 41 percent return above the overall market return. However, the hotel industry in general experienced high returns during this period. If Marriott's returns are measured against the average returns for the six leading hotel chains, Marriott's adjusted return is less than 5 percent for the 12-month period. Some might claim that the spin-off left Marriott share values unchanged.

Performance After the Spin-Off

Both Host Marriott and Marriott International have performed well since the spin-off, whether performance is measured by changes in operations or in shareholder value. As of this writing, neither firm has defaulted on any obligation, and there is no danger of that in the future. Figure 12 shows the growth in value of $1 invested in Marriott in October 1991, with that investment maintained through December 1996. That is, the pro-rata allocations of Host Marriott and Marriott International are held after the spin-off. For comparison purposes, a similar $1 investment in the S&P 500 is also provided. Whereas the S&P 500 investment doubled in value, the Marriott investment increased by a factor of five, with most of the increase coming after the spin-off. Of course, the hotel industry in general experienced good returns over this period, but Marriott shareholders clearly did well.

While the package of stocks representing both Host Marriott and Marriott International offered stellar returns after the spin-off, it is worth noting that both components offered attractive returns. Figure 13 shows the growth of $1 invested in Host Marriott immediately after the spin-off and the growth of $1 invested in Marriott International. Again, both investments are compared with a $1 investment in the S&P 500. While the dollar invested in the S&P 500 grew to about $1.50, the dollar invested in Host Marriott grew to almost $2.50, and the dollar invested in Marriott International grew to about $2.25. The entire package of Marriott shares performed well, but both components contributed.

Improvements in operating performance also were substantial. Table 16 reports figures for sales, income, and earnings per share from before the spin-off through the end of 1995. Not surprisingly, Host Marriott reported negative earnings for two of the three years after the spin-off. This result is influenced by the heavy depreciation charges incurred by firms with large real estate holdings and confirms management's claim that the real estate end of the business was a drag on

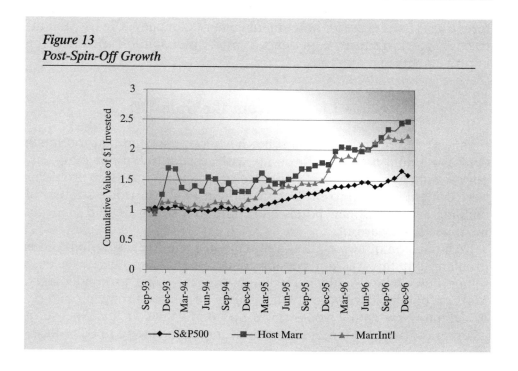

Figure 12
Stock Market Performance of Marriott

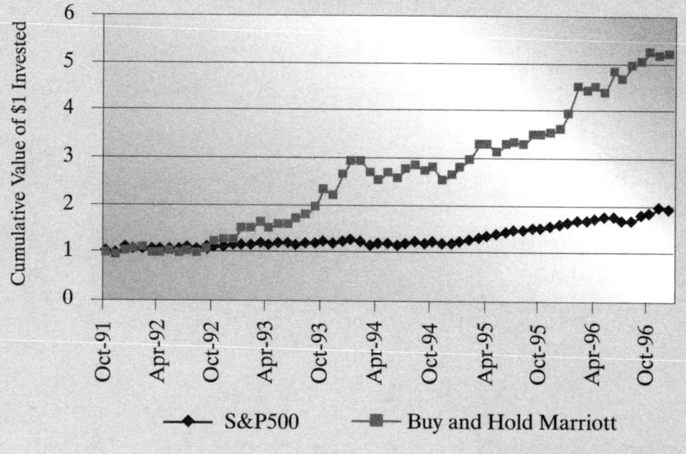

Figure 13
Post-Spin-Off Growth

Table 16
Pre-Spin-Off Performance

Company	Year	Sales (Millions)	Income (Millions)	EPS ($)	Share Price ($)
Marriott Corp.	1991	$8,331	$82	0.80	16.625
Marriott Corp.	1992	$8,722	$85	0.64	20.750
Host Marriott Corp.	1993	$1,791	$57	0.43	9.125
Host Marriott Corp.	1994	$1,501	($19)	-0.13	9.625
Host Marriott Corp.	1995	$484	($62)	-0.39	13.125
Marriott Intl.	1993	$7,430	$159	1.28	29.000
Marriott Intl.	1994	$8,415	$200	1.51	28.125
Marriott Intl.	1995	$8,961	$247	1.87	38.250

corporate earnings. Now, investors can value Host Marriott on its cash flow, as is typically done with real estate companies, while Marriott International is valued as a hotel management company. Clearly, the attractive stock returns experienced after the spin-off parallel the improvements in operations.

Some Lessons from the Spin-Off

Financial theory and common sense have long asserted that too much debt can diminish a firm's flexibility with respect to both ongoing corporate strategy and the firm's ability to raise new capital. Both problems were evident in the Marriott Corporation in 1992. Marriott's strategy of building and selling new hotels had come to a standstill, and management needed a way out.

An infusion of new equity capital might seem like a solution to this problem, but this was not possible under the circumstances, because selling new shares would immediately transfer value to bondholders. Marriott bondholders were holding claims with at least some probability of default. New equity would shore up bond values at the expense of share price. Any announcement that leverage ratios were to be reduced by an infusion of new equity capital would be met with significant declines in share price. This phenomenon is well documented empirically.

The spin-off created two corporate entities with dramatically different leverage ratios. The idea as expressed by Marriott's management is that the debt capacity was reallocated. Since Host Marriott was left with most of the debt, Marriott International could issue new debt and use the proceeds to pursue the strategy of building and selling new hotels. This spin-off exposed bondholders to increased risks of default, as reflected in the decline in bond values after the spin-off announcement. However, in retrospect, this risk led to no defaults because all bondholders were paid in full over the years following the spin-off. The Marriott strategy continued in its separate corporate entities, and shareholder values increased significantly. Whether this was a gamble with bondholder money or a well-calculated business plan might be a matter of debate, but history shows that both bondholders and shareholders profited from this action.

Summary

What

On October 8, 1993, Marriott distributed a stock dividend of shares in its Marriott International subsidiary to its own shareholders. Subsequently, Marriott changed its name to Host Marriott and two independent corporations, Marriott International and Host Marriott, came into existence. For a brief moment at the time of the stock dividend, both firms had identical sets of shareholders, but within an instant of subsequent trading activity, the shareholder groups began to differ. This restructuring is typically called a "spin-off."

Why

Marriott management believed that the hotel real estate business and the services aspects of the business were distinct and could best be managed as separate firms. The spin-off increased corporate focus for both Host Marriott and Marriott International. Also, the original Marriott needed to raise external capital for expansion purposes. Placing most of the debt with the real estate business "reallocated" debt capacity in a manner that allowed the services business to issue new debt at reasonable rates.

Cost

Unlike equity carve-outs and the attending costs associated with the initial public offering, there are virtually no directly observable costs associated with spin-offs. However, the high-level executives we interviewed never failed to mention the large number of hours spent in meetings (either to configure the spin-off or, in this case, to negotiate with Marriott bondholders).

Key Outcomes

Corporate focus is enhanced.

Debt capacity is reallocated, allowing better access to bond markets.

Shareholders were allowed to choose either or both alternative investments in real estate or management.

Results

Shareholders earned remarkable returns over the period including and subsequent to the spin-off.

Operating performance improved substantially.

Summary

S pin-offs and equity carve-outs have been the most popular means of restructuring in the 1990s. Their growing popularity among both corporate executives and researchers stems from increased corporate focus, which enhances both corporate performance and returns to shareholders. Spin-offs and carve-outs sharpen corporate focus in different ways. Restructuring through spin-offs creates two separate corporations with no links to one another after the spin-off, other than prior contractual agreements. With carve-outs, the parent firm usually retains a controlling interest in the subsidiary, but grants a newly created subsidiary board substantial decision-making autonomy.

Based on our interviews with executives, we found that the sharpened focus in organizations (following spin-offs or carve-outs) takes various forms. Without the parent to depend on, the spun-off company finds that the customer becomes more important than ever as the source of capital for survival and growth. Also, urgency for action in product development and marketing is common for companies that are suddenly separated from their parents. Allocating capital, which is truly a scarce resource in these organizations, becomes more centered on economic needs and potential returns and not on political concerns.

In addition, as the Thermo Electron experience demonstrates, the new organization breeds innovation and appropriate risk-taking. In many cases these separations ignite an entrepreneurial spirit focused on success. Finally, employees in the new company now have an unbiased scoreboard in the form of a stock price with which to measure their success.

Spin-offs and carve-outs also allow for more effective executive incentive devices. For our sample of equity carve-outs, 8 percent of the carved-out subsidiaries implemented executive stock option plans at the initial public offering of subsidiary common stock. These stock options depend on just the subsidiary's performance. By contrast, before the equity carve-out, subsidiary executives could only participate in stock option plans based on parent firm shares. It is similar for subsidiaries that become independent corporations through a spin-off. Stock options tied only to subsidiary performance are available for executives after the spin-off, whereas beforehand, stock options would need to be written on parent firm shares.

We generated large samples for spin-offs and equity carve-outs to study changes in operating performance and shareholder value after the restructuring activities. Both spin-offs and carve-outs produce substantial improvements in operations and significant increases in shareholder value. This indicates these vehicles are important tools for improving the efficiency of corporate activities.

For the three years following a spin-off, the average subsidiary outperforms the overall market return by more than 30 percent. The incidence of takeovers among these subsidiaries is very high, so a good portion of these higher returns are from takeover premiums. Similarly, the average parent firm outperforms the market by about 20 percent over the three years following a spin-off. As with the subsidiaries, there is an abnormally high frequency of takeovers among the parent firms in our sample, and we attribute a significant fraction of their high returns to takeover premiums. For the six-month period prior to the spin-offs, the parent firms in our sample outperformed the market by a wide margin, probably because investors anticipate the ensuing spin-off events and the increased profitability that often accompanies them. Nevertheless, our evidence indicates spin-offs substantially enhance shareholder value.

To explain these dramatic increases, we examined changes in operating performance for both the subsidiaries and their parents. For our sample, we calculated average growth rates for sales, operating income, capital expenditures, and total assets. We found that spin-offs outgrow the other firms in their respective industries by a wide margin. When we measured growth rates from one year before the spin-offs to three years after, we found that our average subsidiary had a sales growth rate about 15 percent higher than its competitors. Similar figures for operating income, capital expenditures, and total assets are 24 percent, 39 percent, and 20 percent respectively.

Also interesting to note are the changes in the parent firm's operating performance around the time of a spin-off. From one to three years before the spin-off, our average parent firm exhibited a sales growth rate that is 10 percent less than the growth rate for the average firm in that industry. Our average parent firm showed growth rates for operating income, capital expenditures, and total assets that are also below the average for its industry (–3 percent, –17 percent, and –7 percent, respectively). After the spin-off, the growth rate for these parent firms about equals the industry average. This improvement is likely to contribute to the run-up in share price after the spin-offs.

Our sample of equity carve-outs showed very similar results. Prices increase before the carve-out announcement. After the initial public offering of subsidiary shares, both the average parent firm and the average carve-out performed extremely well in the stock market. We found that subsidiaries show higher growth rates than their competitors for key accounting variables and that parent firms, too, improve in important financial ratios. The correlation between stock market performance and subsequent operating performance was strong. Our study indicated the major source of shareholder gains from equity carve-outs are the subsequent improvements in operating performance.

We interviewed several CFOs and one CEO on restructuring through spin-offs and carve-outs. The executives in the spun-off subsidiaries and the carve-out all emphasized the importance of autonomy and the ability to make decisions unencumbered by the concerns of the parent organization. These executives did not diminish the importance of parent concerns, but they did make clear that certain tradeoffs were present before the divestitute that hampered their ability to maximize the subsidiaries' value.

The parent firms' executives all agreed that these divestitures were good for their organizations. However, these executives did not feel the restructuring affected their parent firms to the same degree as did the subsidiaries' executives. This is to be expected, since the subsidiary in most instances was much smaller than the parent. For example, Photomasks was a very small portion of DuPont, and while the carve-out was very significant for the Photomasks executives, it was rather insignificant for DuPont as a whole. Nevertheless, the DuPont people viewed this carve-out with interest as an experiment on how to wring greater value out of subsidiaries that were underperforming.

In general, divestitures improve returns to shareholders and substantially improve operating performance. Interviews with key executives involved in divestitures indicate that sharpened focus and more independence for subsidiary decision-making are a crucial foundation for these improvements. For equity carve-outs, the parent firm typically retains a controlling interest in the subsidiary, but an independent board can preserve substantial autonomy for the carve-out decision-making process. For spin-offs, the subsidiary becomes a separate free-standing corporation with no ties to the parent firm. Executives also emphasized in our interviews that strengthened financial incentives play an important role in the improvements spin-offs and carve-outs generate. We suspect that as corporations grow even larger over the next decade, spin-offs and equity carve-outs will play an ever-increasing role in maintaining the efficiency of industry.

Interview Protocol

Pre-Spin-off/Equity Carve-Out

Objective/Motivation

- What was the primary motivation for the spin-off/ECO?
- Was there pressure from institutional investors?
- What did you hope to achieve through the spin-off?

Spin-off versus ECO

- What alternatives did you consider before your spin-off/ECO?
- In your case, what were the pros and cons of an ECO before spin-off?
- Why did you choose the one that you did?

Time Line

- Please provide a timeline of the activities leading up to the spin-off/ECO.
- When were the alternative advisors brought in?
- Please list the regulatory filings you filed before the spin-off/ECO.
- What regulatory, accounting, and tax issues did you encounter in your spin-off/ECO?

Valuation and Targeted Stock Price

- Did you hire financial advisors or investment bankers?
- If so, what did they do for you?
- How were the spin-off/ECO shares valued?
- How did you select a targeted stock price range?

Corporate Governance

- When did you establish a board of directors?
- How were members of the board selected for the spin-off/ECO?
- What percentage of the board were outside directors?
- Were any officers added or removed?

Spin-off Capitalization and Division of Liabilities

- Discuss how the capital structure was decided upon.
- Was there a targeted credit rating?
- How were the pension liabilities allocated?
- How were other liabilities allocated between the parent and subsidiary?

Human Resources, Executive Compensation, and Employee Benefits

- Discuss the management selection process for the spin-off/ECO.
- How were managers assigned to the parent or the divested unit?
- Were there any layoffs?
- How was the executive compensation plan designed?

- When were stock options in the spin-off granted?
- What was the strike price?
- Did employee benefits change significantly?

Division of Other Assets

- How were corporate assets allocated between the parent and subsidiary?
- What were the problem areas in the division of assets?

General Questions

- What was the working capital support for the subsidiary?
- Was a line of credit obtained?
- Were there any intellectual property issues?
- How were unionized employees dealt with?
- Which stock exchange was selected for the spin-off/ECO and why?
- Did you have a road show for the spin-off/ECO?

Post Spin-off/ECO Performance

- How did the parent and spin-off/ECO perform in terms of profitability in the first, second, and third year following the spin-off/ECO relative to industry peers?
- How did the common stock of the parent and spin-off/ECO perform in the first, second, and third year following the spin-off/ECO relative to industry peers?
- How did the spin-off/ECO affect the operations of the finance function of the parent and subsidiary?

What changes occurred in the subsidiary as a result of the spin-off/ECO in the following areas:

- Performance measurement and benchmarking
- Organizational structure
- Business and financial strategies
- Capital allocation procedures
- Customer relations and customer focus
- Creating new products and services
- Entering new markets
- The product development process
- Operating efficiencies and quality programs
- Cost cutting/staff reductions
- Corporate culture
- Executive compensation
- International ventures
- Other areas

What factors contributed to the success or failure of the divestiture?

Bibliography

Alexander, Gordon J., P. George Benson, and Joan M. Kampmeyer. 1984. "Investigating the Valuation Effects of Announcements of Voluntary Corporate Selloffs." *The Journal of Finance* 39 (2):503-517.

Aron, Debra J. 1991. "Using the Capital Market as a Monitor: Corporate Spinoffs in an Agency Framework." *The Rand Journal of Economics* 22:505-518.

Asquith, P., and D. Mullins. 1986. "Equity Issues and Offering Dilution." *Journal of Financial Economics* 15:153-186.

Carter, Richard, and Steven Manaster. 1990. "Initial Public Offerings and Underwriter Reputation." *The Journal of Finance* 45 (4):1045-1067.

Cusatis, Patrick J., James A. Miles, and J. Randall Woolridge. 1993. "Restructuring through Spinoffs: The Stock Market Evidence." *Journal of Financial Economics* 33:293-311.

Cusatis, Patrick J., James A. Miles, and J. Randall Woolridge. 1994. "Some New Evidence that Spinoffs Create Value." *Journal of Applied Corporate Finance* 7 (2):100-107.

DeAngelo, Linda E. 1986. "Accounting Numbers as Market Valuation Substitutes." *Accounting Review* 61:400-420.

Demsetz, Harold. 1983. "The Structure of Ownership and the Theory of the Firm." *Journal of Law and Economics* 26 (2):375-390.

Demsetz, Harold, and Kenneth Lehn. 1985. "The Structure of Corporate Ownership: Causes and Consequences." *Journal of Political Economy* 93 (6):1155-1177.

Eaton, Leslie. 1997. "Corporate Spinoffs are Getting a New Spin." *New York Times* (January 30, 1997), p. D-1, 8.

Fama, Eugene F., and Michael C. Jensen. 1983. "Separation of Ownership and Control." *Journal of Law and Economics* 26:301-325.

David M. Glassman. 1988. "Spinoffs and Spin-Outs: Using 'Securitization' to Beat the Bureaucracy." *Journal of Applied Corporate Finance* 1(1988):82-9.

Guttner, Toddi. 1996. "Pick Your Moment—and Catch a Rising Spinoff." *Business Week* (May 13, 1996), pp. 156-7.

Harris, Roy. 1996. "Managing the Downside of the Spinoff Spree." *CFO Magazine* (July 1996), pp. 18-24.

Hearth, Douglas, and Janis K. Zaima. 1984. "Voluntary Corporate Divestitures and Value." *Financial Management* (Spring), 10-16.

Hirschey, Mark, and Janis K. Zaima. 1989. "Insider Trading, Ownership Structure, and the Market Assessment of Corporate Sell-Offs." *The Journal of Finance* 44 (4):971-980.

Hite, Gailen L., and James E. Owers. 1983. "Security Price Reactions Around Corporate Spin-Off Announcements." *Journal of Financial Economics* 12:409-436.

Hite, Gailen L., James E. Owers, and Ronald C. Rogers. 1987. "The Market for Interfirm Asset Sales: Partial Sell-Offs and Total Liquidations." *Journal of Financial Economics* 18:229-252.

Holderness, Clifford G., and Dennis P. Sheehan. 1988. "The Role of Majority Shareholders in Publicly Held Corporations." *Journal of Financial Economics* 20:317-346.

Hudson, Carl D., John S. Jahera, Jr., and William P. Lloyd. 1992. "Further Evidence on the Relationship Between Ownership and Performance." *The Financial Review* 27 (2):227-239.

Hulburt, Heather M., James A. Miles, and J. Randall Woolridge. 1994. "Corporate Restructuring: An Examination of the Effects of Equity Carve-Outs on Firm Performance." Working paper, The Pennsylvania State University, 1997.

Hylton, Richard D. 1995. "If You've Been Burned by IPOs, Take a Look at These." *Fortune* (March 20), 130.

Ibbotson, Roger G., Jody L. Sindelar, and Jay R. Ritter. 1988. "Initial Public Offerings." *Journal of Applied Corporate Finance* 1 (2):37-45.

Jain, Prem C. 1985. "The Effect of Voluntary Sell-Off Announcements on Shareholder Wealth." *The Journal of Finance* 40 (1):209-224.

Jensen, Michael C. 1988. "Agency Costs of Free Cash Flow, Corporate Finance, and the Market for Takeovers." *American Economic Review* 76:323-329.

Jensen, Michael C., and William H. Meckling. 1976. "Theory of the Firm: Managerial Behavior, Agency Costs and Ownership Structure." *Journal of Financial Economics* 3:305-360.

Jensen, Michael C., and Jerold B. Warner. 1988. "The Distribution of Power Among Corporate Managers, Shareholders, and Directors." *Journal of Financial Economics* 20:3-34.

Jongbloed, Auke. 1992. "A Comparison of Spin-Offs and Equity Carve-Outs." Working paper, The University of Rochester.

Kaplan, Steven. 1989. "The Effects of Management Buyouts on Operating Performance and Value." *Journal of Financial Economics* 24:217-254.

Kim, Wi Saeng, Jae Won Lee, and Jack Clark Francis. 1988. "Investment Performance of Common Stocks in Relation to Insider Ownership." *The Financial Review* 23 (1):53-64.

Klein, April. 1986. "The Timing and Substance of Divestiture Announcements: Individual, Simultaneous and Cumulative Effects." *The Journal of Finance* 41 (3):685-696.

Klein, April, James Rosenfeld, and William Beranek. 1991. "The Two Stages of an Equity Carve-Out and the Price Response of Parent and Subsidiary Stock." *Managerial and Decision Economics* 12:449-460.

Korajczyk, Robert, Deborah Lucas, and Rene M. Stulz. 1990. "Understanding Stock Price Behavior Around the Time of Equity Issues."

Asymmetric Information, Corporate Finance, and Investment. R.G. Hubbard, ed. Chicago Press, Chicago.

Lacoursiere, Catherine. 1997. "Spinoffs Start to Sputter." *Treasury and Risk Management Magazine* (January-February, 1997), pp. 28-31.

Lane, Daley, Vikas Mehrotra, and Ranjini Sivakumar. 1997. "Corporate Focus and Value Creation: Evidence from Spinoffs." *Journal of Financial Economics* 45:257-80.

Lang, Larry, Annette Poulsen, and Rene M. Stulz. 1995. "Asset Sales, Firm Performance, and the Agency Costs of Managerial Discretion." *Journal of Financial Economics* 37:3-37.

Lowengood, Mary. 1996. "Secrets of the Spin." *Institutional Investor* (December 1996), pp. 36-7.

Lowenstein, Roger. 1996. "Confessions of a Corporate Spinoff Junkie." *Wall Street Journal* (March 28, 1996), p. C1.

Masulis, Ronald W., and Ashok N. Korwar. 1986. "Seasoned Equity Offerings: An Empirical Investigation." *Journal of Financial Economics* 15:91-118.

McConnell, John J., and Henri Servaes. 1990. "Additional Evidence on Equity Ownership and Corporate Value." *Journal of Financial Economics* 277:595-612.

Michels, Antony J., and Shelley Neumeier. 1994. "Spiffy Returns from Spinoffs." *Fortune* (April 18), 31-32.

Michaely, Roni, and Wayne Shaw. 1995. "The Choice of Going Public: Spinoffs vs. Carve-Outs." *Financial Management* (Autumn 1995), pp. 5-21.

Mikkelson, Wayne, and Megan Partch. 1986. "Valuation Effects of Security Offerings and the Issuance Process." *Journal of Financial Economics* 15:31-60.

Miles, James A., and James D. Rosenfeld. 1983. "The Effect of Voluntary Spin-Off Announcements on Shareholder Wealth." *The Journal of Finance* 38 (5):1597-1606.

Miles, James A., J. Randall Woolridge, and Michael J. Woolfolk. 1994. "An Empirical Analysis of Taxable Stock Distributions: The Effect of Tax and Regulatory Actions in Informationally Asymmetric Markets." Working paper, The Pennsylvania State University.

Morck, Randall, Andrei Shleifer, and Robert W. Vishny. 1988. "Management Ownership and Market Valuation: An Empirical Analysis." *Journal of Financial Economics* 20:293-315.

Muscarella, Chris J., and Michael R. Vetsuypens. 1989. "A Simple Test of Baron's Model of IPO Underpricing." *Journal of Financial Economics* 24:125-135.

Muscarella, Chris J., and Michael R. Vetsuypens. 1990. "Efficiency and Organizational Structure: A Study of Reverse LBOs." *The Journal of Finance* 45 (5):1389-1413.

Myers, Stewart, and Nicholas Majluf. 1984. "Corporate Financing and Investment Decisions When Firms Have Information that Investors Do Not Have." *Journal of Financial Economics* 13:187-221.

Nanda, Vikram. 1991. "On the Good News in Equity Carve-Outs." *The Journal of Finance* 46 (5):1717-1736.

Parrino, Robert. 1997. "Spinoffs and Wealth Transfers: The Marriott Case." *Journal of Financial Economics* (February 1997), pp. 241-274.

Perlmuth, Lyn. 1997. "Craving for Carveouts." *Institutional Investor* (February 1997), p. 35.

Rehfeld, Barry. 1996. "Good Riddance." *Institutional Investor* (October 1996), pp. 183-4.

Ritter, Jay R. 1984. "The 'Hot Issue' Market of 1980." *Journal of Business* 57 (2):215-240.

Ritter, Jay R. 1987. "The Costs of Going Public." *Journal of Financial Economics* 19:269-281.

Ritter, Jay R. 1991. "The Long-Run Performance of Initial Public Offerings." *The Journal of Finance* 46 (1):3-27.

Roll, Richard. 1983. "On Computing Mean Returns and the Small Firm Premium." *Journal of Financial Economics* 12:371-386.

Rosenfeld, James D. 1984. "Additional Evidence on the Relation Between Divestiture Announcements and Shareholder Wealth." *The Journal of Finance* 39 (5):1437-1448.

Ryan, Kevin. 1996. "From Spinoff to Success." *Wall Street Journal* (May 27, 1996), p. A-18.

Salomon Brothers. 1994. *The Issuer's Guide to Equity Carve-Outs* (July 1994).

Satler, David, Andrew Campbell, and Richard Koch. 1997. *Break Up! How Companies Use Spinoffs to Gain Focus and Grow Strong.* The Free Press, New York.

Schipper, Katherine, and Abbie Smith. 1983. "Effects of Recontracting on Shareholder Wealth: The Case of Voluntary Spin-Offs." *Journal of Financial Economics* 12:437-467.

Schipper, Katherine, and Abbie Smith. 1986. "A Comparison of Equity Carve-Outs and Seasoned Equity Offerings." *Journal of Financial Economics* 15:153-186.

Seward, James, and James Walsh. 1996. "The Governance and Control of Voluntary Corporate Spinoffs." *Strategic Management Journal* 17:25-39.

Slovin, Myron B., and Marie E. Sushka. 1993. "Ownership Concentration, Corporate Control Activity, and Firm Value: Evidence from the Death of Inside Blockholders." *The Journal of Finance* 48 (4): 1293-1321.

Slovin, Myron B., Marie E. Sushka, and Steven R. Ferraro. 1995. "A Comparison of the Information Conveyed by Equity Carve-Outs, Spin-Offs, and Asset Sell-Offs." *Journal of Financial Economics* 37:89-104.

Smith, Abbie J. 1990. "Corporate Ownership Structure and Performance: The Case of Management Buyouts." *Journal of Financial Economics* 27:143-164.

Smith, Clifford W., Jr. 1986. "Investment Banking and the Capital Acquisition Process." *Journal of Financial Economics* 15:3-29.

"Spinning it Out at Thermo Electron." 1997. *The Economist,* April 12, 1997, pp. 57-8.

Stulz, Rene M. 1988. "Managerial Control of Voting Rights: Financing Policies and the Market for Corporate Control." *Journal of Financial Economics* 20:25-54.

Sturm, Paul. "Picking Up the Pieces." *Smart Money,* October 1996, pp. 65-6.

Tinic, Seha. 1988. "Anatomy of Initial Public Offerings of Common Stock." *The Journal of Finance* 43 (4):789-822.

Wilke, John R. 1993. "Thermo Electron Uses an Unusual Strategy to Create Products." *Wall Street Journal,* August 5, 1993, p. A-1.

James A. Miles is the Joseph F. Bradley Fellow of Finance at The Pennsylvania State University. His teaching and research interests are in corporate finance and investments, with an emphasis on the effects of compensation structure on corporate decisionmaking. He has published over 25 articles in leading academic and professional journals, including the *Journal of Finance, Journal of Financial Economics, Journal of Law and Economics,* and the *Journal of the American Statistical Association.* Dr. Miles' research has been highlighted extensively in the financial press. He has been quoted in *Fortune,* the *New York Times, Forbes, The Economist, Financial World, Barron's,* the *Wall Street Journal, Business Week,* the *Washington Post, CFO Magazine, Investors' Business Daily, Worth Magazine, USA Today,* and other publications for his work in the area of divestitures. His research on rights offerings was featured in a recent *Barron's* column. Professor Miles served for five years as an associate editor of *Financial Management,* the journal of the Financial Management Association.

J. Randall Woolridge is the Goldman, Sachs & Co. and Frank P. Smeal Endowed University Fellow in Finance at The Pennsylvania State University. His teaching and research interests are in corporate finance, with an emphasis on the valuation consequences of corporate strategic investment and financial decisions. He has published over 25 articles in leading academic and professional journals, including *Journal of Finance, Journal of Financial Economics, Strategic Management Journal,* and the *Harvard Business Review.* Dr. Woolridge's research has been highlighted extensively in the financial press. He has been quoted in *Fortune,* the *New York Times, Forbes, The Economist, Financial World, Barron's,* the *Wall Street Journal, Business Week,* the *Washington Post, CFO Magazine, Investors' Business Daily, Worth Magazine, USA Today,* and other publications. In addition, Dr. Woolridge has appeared on CNN's *Money Line* and CNBC's *Business Today.* He has participated in executive development programs in more than 20 countries in North and South America, Europe, and Asia and has consulted with corporations, investment banks, and government agencies.

ACKNOWLEDGMENTS

This research project has benefited from the help of numerous individuals. We thank Jim Lewis and Bill Sinnett of FERF for their assistance (and prodding). We also thank the many executives who helped us with our cases involving spin-offs and equity carve-outs. We especially want to thank Larry Prendergast of AT&T Investment Management Corp., Paul Hayes and Peter Sperling of Lucent Technologies, Neil Bunis of DuPont, Mike Hardinger of DuPont Photomasks, Mike Stein of Nordstrom, Inc., and Robert Parsons of Host Marriott. We also appreciate the efforts of our former Ph.D. students—Patrick Cusatis of First Union National Bank and Heather Hurlbut of the University of West Virginia—who worked with us on spin-offs and equity carve-outs. Finally, we want to thank Robert Parrino, whose *Journal of Financial Economics* paper (February 1997) provided much of the data pertaining to the Marriott spin-off. Of course, only the authors are responsible for any errors, and we hope there are few of them.